Abigail Adams

Abigail
Adams

Kem Knapp Sawyer

DK PUBLISHING

LONDON, NEW YORK, MUNICH,
MELBOURNE, AND DELHI

Editor : Beth Landis Hester
Publishing Director : Beth Sutinis
Designer : Mark Johnson Davies
Managing Art Editor : Michelle Baxter
Production Controller : Jen Lockwood
DTP Coordinator : Kathy Farias
Photo Research : Anne Burns Images

First American Edition, 2009

09 10 11 12 13 10 9 8 7 6 5 4 3 2 1
Published in the United States
by DK Publishing
375 Hudson Street
New York, New York 10014

DK books are available at special discounts
when purchased in bulk for sales promotions,
premiums, fund-raising,
or educational use. For details, contact:

DK Publishing Special Markets
375 Hudson Street
New York, New York 10014
SpecialSales@dk.com

A catalog record for this book is available
from the Library of Congress.

ISBN 978-0-7566-5209-8 (Paperback)
ISBN 978-0-7566-5208-1 (Hardcover)

Printed and bound in China
by South China Printing Co., Ltd.

Discover more at
www.dk.com

Contents

Prologue

A Decisive Day

"Charlestown is laid in ashes," Abigail wrote. "The constant roar of the cannon is so distressing that we cannot eat, drink, or sleep." The bloody Battle of Bunker Hill raged on.

The American colonists, angry that they paid taxes but had no voice in government, were pitted against the British. Their protests had been ignored, and they had chosen freedom, no matter what the cost. They would fight for the rights the British had denied them.

Abigail, a young mother, and her seven-year-old son, Johnny, climbed up the rocks at Penn Hill, not far from their home. Standing on top of the steep mound, they could look out over

General Joseph Warren was killed by a musket ball at the Battle of Bunker Hill, depicted here by artist John Trumbull.

the water of Boston Harbor and see Charlestown, still in flames, in the distance. They could even smell the smoke and soot. Houses burned, women and children fled, soldiers were wounded, and many died.

But Abigail knew no fear; she reached out to those in need, friends who had escaped from Boston, where the British had laid siege. The orphans left behind by a fallen friend were camped out at her house.

Abigail's husband, John, was in Philadelphia, serving as a member of the Second Continental Congress. Delegates from the 13 American colonies attended. All of them wanted to ensure the people's right to govern themselves.

John's work would keep him away from home for months at a time, so it fell to Abigail to look after their four children and manage the family farm. Still, she found time to write to John and report on the state of affairs in Massachusetts, where the struggle for independence had begun. After the Battle of Bunker Hill, Abigail wrote to John, "The day—perhaps the decisive day—is come, on which the fate of America depends."

Both Abigail and John believed deeply in this cause. It was important to them that Americans break away from Britain and enjoy the rights of free citizens. John and the other delegates had acted boldly, putting the lives of their countrymen at risk by voting for independence. Abigail wanted to reassure her husband. "The spirits of the people are very good," she wrote. "The loss of Charlestown affects them no more than a drop in the bucket."

chapter 1
A New England Childhood

W illiam Smith, the son of a Boston merchant, had studied theology at Harvard College. In 1734, he was called to be the

PARSONAGE

A parsonage is a residence provided by the church for the use of a parson, or minister.

minister of the North Parish Church in Weymouth, a small coastal town 13 miles (21 km) from Boston. He moved into the parsonage and bought several acres of land. Like most ministers in the area, he not only looked after the parish, but also became a farmer.

William soon married Elizabeth Quincy, who came from a prominent family in the neighboring town of Braintree.

All four of Elizabeth and William's children were born at the Weymouth parsonage.

She had grown up at Mount Wollaston, an estate that overlooked the sea and was one of the largest in the town. The Quincys were well known throughout the community—Elizabeth's father had served in the Massachusetts legislature and as a justice of the peace. William and Elizabeth's daughter Abigail was born on November 22, 1744, the second of four children. Mary was the oldest, and William and Elizabeth were younger.

Harvard College

Harvard College was founded in 1636 by an act of the Massachusetts Bay Colony legislature. It was named for John Harvard, a Charlestown minister, who had bequeathed his library to the college. When it first opened its doors to nine students and one teacher, the academic curriculum stressed the classics, ancient texts of Greece and Rome. Many New England ministers would be trained here.

Elizabeth taught her daughters to cook and sew at a very young age. By the time she was five, Abigail was expected to do daily chores. Her mother was a kind, generous-spirited woman, giving instructions in weaving to the women in the parish and helping them sell their handiwork. She did not enter into parish quarrels and often visited the sick with Abigail at her side. On Sundays, the routine changed: William would

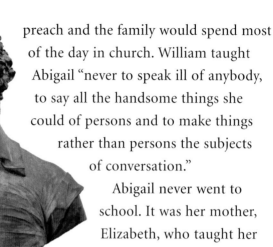

preach and the family would spend most of the day in church. William taught Abigail "never to speak ill of anybody, to say all the handsome things she could of persons and to make things rather than persons the subjects of conversation."

Abigail never went to school. It was her mother, Elizabeth, who taught her the letters of the alphabet as well as simple arithmetic. Later her father, William, introduced her to the many books in his library, a large collection that

This bust of William Shakespeare was created by John Michael Rysbrack. Abigail spent hours reading Shakespeare's plays and sonnets in her father's library.

included several hundred volumes. Abigail was eager to read and discuss each book. She studied Shakespeare and the Bible, she memorized poetry by John Milton and Alexander Pope, and she read novels by Laurence Sterne and Jonathan Swift.

Some of Abigail's friends had learned to read in a dame school. The boys would later go on to elementary school; some prepared for college in a grammar school or with a tutor. Fewer opportunities were available to girls. Some schools offered a couple of classes for

DAME SCHOOL

At a dame school, an educated woman would hold classes for local children in her home.

girls at odd hours. Wealthier parents might hire tutors to give their daughters lessons in French, music, painting,

"Make things rather than persons the subject of conversation."

–William Smith's advice to his daughter Abigail

history, and literature. But many girls never received a formal education.

Since Abigail was often ill with colds and fevers, her parents thought she would fare better at home than in a schoolhouse. She learned as much about literature and history as other children did at school. Her parents were pleased with her progress, but worried that she spent too much time with her books.

Abigail, like many children in New England, stayed with relatives for several weeks at a time, forming deep bonds and gaining new experiences. She especially liked going to Boston to see her aunt and uncle. Boston, home to the governor of Massachusetts, with a busy port and market, was much more exciting than Weymouth. Abigail also looked forward to visiting her grandparents and was always made to feel comfortable in their home. Her mother sometimes scolded her for being too strong-willed, but Grandmother Quincy never criticized. Abigail would inherit her grandmother's "lively, cheerful disposition" and, like her grandmother, would learn to mix "instruction and amusement."

Massachusetts (in yellow) is in the center of this map of New England. Edmund Quincy, Abigail's ancestor, settled there in 1633. Five years later, John Adams's ancestor Henry Adams arrived.

Although Abigail visited relatives when she was young, her frequent illnesses prevented her from playing with children her own age. Later, her grandson Charles Adams would write that it was this seclusion from her peers that helped produce "a meditative, imaginative mind." But as a teenager, Abigail became more outgoing, developed deep friendships, and started a habit she would keep as long as she lived: writing letters to friends. She discussed philosophical—as well as trivial—matters with her cousin Isaac, her aunt's sister Hannah, and her friend Polly. They wrote about politics and daily activities, often using pen names. Abigail called herself "Diana," the Roman goddess of the moon and hunt. One friend was "Calliope," the Greek muse of eloquence, and another was "Silvia," a Roman shepherdess.

At the age of 15, Abigail met a young man named John Adams at a party, but neither one paid much attention to the other. Three years later, John's good friend, the scholarly Richard Cranch, began to call on Abigail's sister Mary. John often accompanied Richard on his visits to the Weymouth parsonage. An articulate lawyer, John was quick to speak his mind—something Abigail found quite attractive. The two would have very lively conversations. Soon, John was coming by himself to see Abigail, and often bringing her books to read. After Mary and Richard's wedding in 1762, John and Abigail discussed marriage, but Abigail was only 18 and they decided to wait.

John rode on horseback the five miles (8 km) along the coast from Braintree to Weymouth as often as he could. He and Abigail shared a passion for learning, an interest in politics, and a witty sense of humor. When they were apart, they used pen and paper to flirt, to tease, and to fall in love.

Not everyone approved of the developing relationship. Abigail's father was suspicious of lawyers and would have preferred his daughter to marry a minister. William did his best to make John feel unwelcome: When the young lawyer came to visit, William would not let him keep his horse in the barn, but made him tie it to a tree by the side of the road. Yet nothing William could do would stop Abigail and John from seeing each other.

chapter **2**

John

John became such a regular visitor to the Smiths' home
that Abigail's parents grew accustomed to his presence and
no longer opposed the match. Abigail and John were married
on October 25, 1764. Abigail, almost 20, was quite thin, only
five feet (152 cm) tall, with long dark brown hair and brown
eyes. John, nine years older, was seven inches (18 cm) taller
than Abigail, slightly plump, with a rounder face and blue
eyes. The simple ceremony took place in the parsonage and
was performed by Abigail's father, William. That afternoon,
Abigail and John moved into their new home—a 100-year-
old house John had inherited from his father. It was just off
the Old Coast Road frequented by travelers on their way
from Boston to Plymouth.

John and Abigail Adams
lived in the house on the
right. John was born in
the house on the left.

SELECTMAN
A selectman is a town official elected to oversee local affairs.

John and his two brothers had grown up in the house next door. His father, also named John, had been a farmer and a shoemaker, as well as a selectman and a church deacon. His mother, Susanna Boylston, came from a well-to-do Braintree family. Their house, built in 1681, had two rooms downstairs and two rooms above. John and Susanna added a room in the back with a sloping roof, called a "lean-to." They used this room, which could hold as many as 23 chairs, for town and church meetings.

Young John learned to read both at home and at school. He enjoyed playing with hoops, marbles, and quoits as well as wrestling, swimming, and skating. He also loved to explore the countryside. Early on, his parents wanted him to go to college and become a minister. When John told them he wanted to be a farmer instead, his father sent him into the fields to work from sunrise to sunset. John did not take to farming.

Joseph Marsh, the master of a nearby boarding school, was chosen to prepare John for Harvard College. John studied hard and came to admire Master Marsh. He was "thunderstruck" when he learned Master Marsh was too ill to accompany him to Cambridge to take the admissions exam. Nevertheless, John made the trip on his own, did well on the exam, and was admitted. His father sold a piece of land to help finance his education—John would also receive

QUOITS
The object of the game called quoits is to throw rings, made of metal or rope, over a post.

Saltbox Houses

"Saltbox houses" like Abigail and John's were popular in Massachusetts. Their name refers to the sloping roof that makes the house resemble a kind of wooden box used at the time to store salt. Saltbox houses had two stories in the front but only one in the back—a trick devised to avoid paying extra taxes on a two-story house.

a scholarship to cover part of the cost.

In 1751, John entered Harvard College at the age of 15. Most of the students were a little older than John, but one student was only 12. In his autobiography, John later wrote that it was in college that he discovered a "growing curiosity, a love of books and a fondness for study." John Winthrop, a well-known astronomer and professor of mathematics and natural philosophy, had a profound influence on John's education. The professor's love of learning was contagious. While taking his courses, John started a diary to record the weather. Later, he would record other thoughts as well, writing about his classes and philosophical issues such as the definition of wisdom or the nature of genius. He would keep a diary for much of his life.

When John joined a debating club at Harvard, he learned he had a gift for public speaking. He considered a career as a minister or scientist, but eventually he chose law instead. After graduation, John moved to Worcester, where he

INFLUENZA

Influenza, or flu, is an infectious and sometimes fatal disease.

rented a room from a physician. He taught school by day and read law books at night. In 1758, he started a law practice in Braintree, taking on many clients from all over Massachusetts. Three years later, his father died from a severe case of influenza. It was a heavy and unexpected loss. The memory of his hardworking father would stay with John for the rest of his life.

When John and Abigail settled into their new house, John kept up his law practice and used one of the front rooms for an office, adding an outside door for clients and law clerks. The parlor, John's law office, and the kitchen were all downstairs. Upstairs were two bed chambers and two small rooms under the eaves. Abigail spent most of her time in the parlor and the kitchen. Judah, a servant who had worked for John's mother, helped with the housework, but

John added an outside door to his office so that his clients could come and go without disturbing the rest of the family.

Abigail's Kitchen

Abigail's kitchen had all the modern conveniences of the 18th century. Heavy cast-iron pots and pans hung from hooks above the large brick fireplace. Carved into the side of the fireplace was an oven in the shape of a beehive, where Abigail baked bread and cakes. She roasted meats on a spit in the fire or in her "tin kitchen"— a small metal contraption that reflected heat. Fruits and vegetables were kept cool in the root cellar. Flour, sugar, and other dry goods were stored in the buttery, a small room off the kitchen.

Abigail did much of it herself. She cooked, baked, churned butter, and preserved foods for winter. Abigail's mother had taught her to spin and sew, and she put those skills to good use, making her own clothes and curtains.

John had inherited not only the house, but also a farm. He and Abigail grew pumpkins, potatoes, and squash, and raised sheep and chickens. The cider they drank came from the apples in their orchards. Their cows produced milk and their forests provided wood for the fire. Since John was busy with his law practice, Abigail looked after the farm. Although the farm met many of their needs, Abigail did buy some supplies from other local farmers, and sugar and molasses from merchants in Boston. White flour for cakes and pies came from New York or Philadelphia.

On July 14, 1765, nine months after they were married, Abigail gave birth to a baby girl. That very day, John took the infant to church in a horse-drawn carriage to have her baptized. The proud parents named her Abigail Amelia and called her "Nabby" for short. She was a good-natured baby with a sweet temper.

During these early days of marriage, John and Abigail, always interested in politics, were becoming more outspoken about their views and their discontent. When the British passed the Stamp Act in 1765, the colonists started to grumble. John published his opinions on the matter in the *Boston Gazette* and was one of the key authors of the "Braintree Instructions." This resolution, adopted by 40 towns, declared that the Stamp Act was burdensome and unconstitutional and that "no freeman should be subject to any tax to which he has not given his own consent."

Although the Stamp Act was repealed in 1766, Britain tightened its control over the colonies by passing the Declaratory Act, giving

The Stamp Act of 1765

The Stamp Act, passed by the British Parliament, required American colonists to buy official stamps to place on every printed legal document, pamphlet, or newspaper. Publishers found ways to express their displeasure; this issue of the *Pennsylvania Journal* shows a skull-and-crossbones in place of the official stamp.

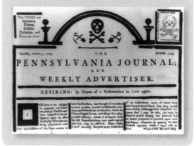

the British Parliament absolute authority to pass laws for the colonies. The Townshend Acts followed in 1767, imposing taxes on the sale of paper, glass, paint, and oil. John joined the Sons of Liberty, a secret society dedicated to resisting British control, and he discussed politics at the Monday Night Club, a group that met in Boston coffeehouses. Abigail remained in Braintree but she was always eager to hear John's reports as soon as he returned.

After the birth of their first son, John Quincy, on July 11, 1767, John and Abigail made the decision to move to Boston. John would be closer to his work there and have more time to spend with his family. Abigail looked forward to being near her Boston friends—as well as her sister Mary. The Adamses rented

Bostonians were outraged to learn of the Stamp Act, which became effective on November 1, 1765.

a house on Brattle Square, only two blocks from Faneuil Hall, the city's main market. John and Abigail's second daughter was born at the Brattle Square house on December 28, 1768, and baptized at Brattle Street Church on New Year's Day. They named her Susanna after John's mother and called her "Suky." She was small and frail, and Abigail spent most of her time looking after the baby.

Abigail and John sat for these portraits by Benjamin Blyth in August 1766, while spending a week with Abigail's sister Mary and her husband, Richard, in Salem, a seaport north of Boston.

But Abigail also found time to entertain at home. Among the family's friends were Samuel Adams, John's second cousin, and his wife Betsy; John Hancock, a wealthy merchant from Braintree; Josiah Quincy, Abigail's cousin; and Joseph Warren, the family physician. Heated political discussions were common—both Abigail and John were opinionated.

Still, Abigail worried about her daughter Suky. No matter how hard Abigail tried to feed and care for her, Suky would not gain weight. She died on February 4, 1770, at the age of 13 months. Abigail, now five months pregnant, was heartbroken, and John, also deeply upset, preferred not to speak about it. The remainder of Abigail's pregnancy was emotionally difficult. But, on May 29, a healthy baby boy was born. They named him Charles.

Meanwhile, there were more than 4,000 British troops in Boston, and tension between the soldiers and the city's inhabitants was increasing. Around noon on March 5, 1770, bells rang out to signal an alarm. John ran outside to determine the cause and quickly learned that a riot was brewing. Angry Bostonians were throwing oyster shells, small rocks, and chunks of ice at British soldiers. In an event that became

British ships occupy Boston Harbor in 1768.

Capital of New-England ; and of the Landing of —— Troops in the Year 1768, in Confequence of Letters from Gov. Bernard, the Commiffioners, &c. to the Britifh Miniftry.

A Profpective View of the Town of Boston, the

P. REVERE.

1 Beaver.——2 Senegal.——3 Martin.——4 Glafgow.——5 Mermaid.——6 Romney.——7 Lanceflon.——8 Bonetta.

Paul Revere engraved, produced, and sold this print of the Boston Massacre, copied from a drawing by Henry Pelham.

known as the Boston Massacre, the soldiers opened fire, and five men were killed.

The British soldiers were soon put on trial, but no lawyer wanted to represent them. John felt strongly that every person was entitled to a fair trial, regardless of the circumstances. He took the case and agreed to represent the soldiers. John made a forceful argument that the soldiers were acting in self-defense, and the jury found six of the eight soldiers not guilty. The captain was also freed, because it could not be proved that he had given the order to fire.

Before the trial, John had gained the respect of the colonists. He took on the defense of the British soldiers knowing that the choice would be an unpopular one and might damage his reputation. Yet, to his and Abigail's surprise, Bostonians did not hold this against him—in fact, their admiration for him would only grow. In June 1770, John was elected as a representative to the Massachusetts legislature, receiving 418 of the 536 votes.

chapter **3**

Seeds of Revolution

With the strain of the trial and his newly elected position, John was soon suffering from exhaustion. The Adamses returned to Braintree with hopes that the country air and opportunities for exercise would benefit the entire family. In time, John's health improved.

Unfortunately, so much of John's work took place in Boston that he was frequently away from home, leaving Abigail to care for the children and the farm. On September 15, 1772, Abigail gave birth to a third son, Thomas Boylston. Two months later, the family returned to Boston, where Abigail and John met regularly with friends who shared their political interests. In the spring of 1773, Abigail was introduced to Mercy Otis Warren, a woman who would greatly influence her political thinking. In the months and years ahead, the two women would trade sharp-witted opinions on literature, education, history, and government.

Around this time, the political situation in Boston again started heating up. Although Parliament repealed most of the colonial

It is claimed that several generations of the Adams family, including John and his children, were rocked to sleep in this cradle.

Mercy Otis Warren (1728–1814)

As the daughter of a judge, Mercy Otis developed an interest in politics at an early age. Her older brother James helped found the Sons of Liberty, and when Mercy married her brother's friend James Warren, their home in Boston became a meeting place for leading revolutionary thinkers. She later wrote a popular history of the American Revolution. Unfortunately, Abigail Adams believed her friend had misrepresented John's role, and their relationship cooled. In 1812, they would resume their correspondence—and their friendship.

taxes, it had kept in place a tax on tea. In response, Americans planned to boycott the tea. As a further sign of protest, a group of indignant Bostonians, dressed as Indians, boarded a British ship under cover of night, and dumped its cargo of tea into the sea. Although John and Abigail supported the protesters, they knew serious consequences would follow. In retaliation for what became known as the Boston Tea Party

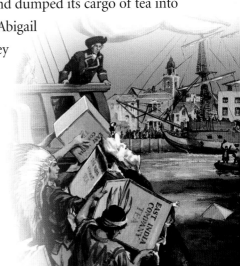

On December 16, 1773, angry American colonists throw crates of British tea into Boston Harbor.

Cartographer Matthew Albert Lotter produced this map of North America around 1776. The 13 British colonies are hand-colored.

the British closed the port of Boston so that Americans could no longer receive many of the goods they needed. Living in Boston became increasingly difficult. In 1774, the Adamses again returned to Braintree.

That summer, while John's legal practice took him away from home, he and Abigail wrote letters exchanging their views on the future of the colonies. "It is a fundamental, inherent and inalienable right of the people, that they have some check, influence, or control in their supreme legislature. If the right of taxation is conceded to Parliament, the Americans have no check or influence at all left," John wrote in one letter. "Great things are wanted to be done, and little things only I fear can be done. I dread the thought of the Congress' falling short of the expectations of the continent, but especially of the people of this province."

John was elected a delegate to the First Continental Congress

"Great things are wanted to be done."

–John Adams, in a letter to Abigail Adams

and, on August 10, 1774, he set out by coach for Philadelphia where the meeting would convene. Abigail stayed behind with the children in Braintree, but knowing John would play an active role in politics gave her great pleasure. "Your task is difficult and important," she wrote. "Heaven direct and prosper you."

First Continental Congress

The First Continental Congress included 56 delegates from 12 of the 13 colonies. (Georgia did not send any delegates.) Its purpose was to plan a course of action in response to various acts of the British Parliament. Eventually, the Congress published a list of rights and grievances and sent a petition to King George III, asking him to respond.

Abigail and John had been separated earlier in their marriage, but John had never traveled this far. "The great distance," Abigail wrote on August 19, "makes the time appear very long. It seems already a month since you left me." She looked forward to their reunion: "The tenderest regard evermore awaits you from your most affectionate Abigail Adams."

Carpenter's Hall in Philadelphia was the meeting place of the First Continental Congress, from September 5 to October 26, 1774.

During the day, Abigail stayed busy caring for the four children, running the household, and managing the farm. But at night, once the children were tucked in bed, she grew lonely. She could not sleep and spent the long evenings writing letters to John. It was at night that Abigail could share her concerns, offer advice, and open her heart.

Much of John and Abigail's letter writing was devoted to the children and their education. Both parents were determined that their children should excel. Abigail asked Johnny to read one or two pages from a book of ancient history aloud to her, hoping he would "entertain a fondness for it." John replied that he was very pleased to hear this and that "the education of our children is never out of my mind." He urged Abigail to "fire them with ambition to be useful" and to encourage them to work hard for that which was "great and solid," not "little and frivolous." He wanted Abigail to teach them grace and honesty, as well as French. Most of John's letters ended with affectionate messages for the children: "My babes are never out of my mind, nor absent from my heart."

Abigail also discussed the ongoing drought, and other matters related to the farm. Both she and John worried about their finances. They knew they had to be frugal in order to make ends meet. John asked his family to spend less so they would have more to give to others. In one letter he hoped that both ladies and gentlemen would commit to wear fewer ornaments, eat potatoes, and drink water. Abigail continued to be as self-sufficient as possible—spinning, weaving, and growing her own fruits and vegetables.

John, however, did not always find it easy to economize. Although he said he would try not to spend so much on books, he continued to expand his library.

In his writing, John also reported on the proceedings of the First Continental Congress. He much admired the other delegates and their public spirit: "There is in the Congress a collection of the greatest men upon this continent in point of abilities, virtues, and fortunes." Worried about those he had left behind, John advised Abigail, "If there is distress and danger in Boston, pray invite our friends, as many as possible, to take an asylum with you."

Abigail kept John informed of every step the British made in Massachusetts. The royal governor seemed increasingly to be preparing for war: mounting cannons on Beacon Hill, digging entrenchments, and assigning regiments to the area.

Abigail wrote long letters by candlelight; she discussed the children, the farm, and the political situation.

ASYLUM

Asylum refers to a shelter or safe place.

When John heard that the British had occupied Boston, he worried about the books and papers he had left there. He asked Abigail to bring all his books and papers to Braintree, then added yet another request: "Tell all my clerks to mind their books and study hard, for their country will stand in need of able counselors."

"I long impatiently to have you upon the stage of action," Abigail said to John. Believing that John was a key player in the struggle for independence made the separation easier to bear. On September 22, 1774, Abigail wrote, "The maxim 'In time of peace prepare for war' (if this may be called a time of peace) resounds throughout the country." John answered that the people should follow the maxim, adding, "But let them avoid war if possible— if possible, I say."

Abigail often scolded John for not writing more frequently. But John had to be cautious about what he wrote. Letters were frequently intercepted and could be read by the British. He explained that he was

Delegates to the First Continental Congress discussed a boycott of British goods as well as a new system of government.

also consumed with work: "My time is totally filled from the moment I get out of bed until I return to it. Visits, ceremonies, company, business, newspapers, pamphlets, etc., etc., etc."

"I long impatiently to have you upon the stage of action."

–Abigail Adams, in a letter to John Adams

John's letters were often delayed because he preferred to trust them to friends rather than pay for the postal service. When five weeks had passed without a letter, Abigail grew exasperated and said she learned more about John's whereabouts from newspapers than from his letters. "I had rather give a dollar for a letter by the post, though the consequence should be that I ate but one meal a day these three weeks to come," she wrote.

Abigail believed John was dealing with the most important issues of the day and that he'd been called to accomplish a task with far-reaching consequences for generations to come. Yet John grew weary of the process and found the affairs of Congress to be "tedious beyond expression." Because every man was a great orator, every man had to show his oratorical skill, and every little point was subject to debate.

After almost three months in Philadelphia, John was ready to come home. He left the city at the end of October 1774, after Congress adjourned. Abigail, eager to see him, asked that once he arrived in Braintree he not spend one hour in town until he had spent twelve with her.

chapter 4

"Dearest Friend"

The first battles of the American Revolution were fought 20 miles (32 km) from Braintree. In April 1775, Dr. Joseph Warren, John and Abigail's friend, learned that British soldiers planned to march through Lexington on their way to Concord to raid stockpiles of American ammunition. He asked the silversmith Paul Revere to alert a miltia group known as the "minutemen." On April 18, Revere made his now-famous midnight ride to Lexington to warn the minutemen that the British were coming.

British soldiers did indeed march to Lexington. But when they arrived, American militiamen were waiting for them

Paul Revere (1735–1818)

Like John Adams, Paul Revere was a member of the Sons of Liberty. Before starting on his midnight ride, Revere had two lanterns hung in the steeple of the Old North Church in Boston, a signal that the British were crossing the Charles River. His journey to alert the minutemen later became the subject of Henry Wadsworth Longfellow's poem, "Paul Revere's Ride," which contained many historical inaccuracies.

on the village green. Shots were fired at sunrise, and eight Americans died. The British moved on to Concord and

Led by Captain John Parker, 77 militiamen fought in the Battle of Lexington on April 19, 1775.

another battle ensued. Although they captured some of the American ammunition, the British eventually withdrew in defeat after several of their troops were killed or wounded.

That May, John returned to Philadelphia as a delegate to the Second Continental Congress. This time Congress voted to create an official Continental Army and unanimously elected military hero George Washington as commander. John wrote to Abigail, concerned about her safety. He warned her not to fear imaginary danger, but "in case of real danger," he wrote, "fly to the woods with our children." Abigail, in turn, worried about John's well-being: "I felt very anxious about you; though I endeavored to be very insensible and heroic, yet my heart felt like a heart of lead."

After watching the Battle of Bunker Hill from afar, John Quincy wrote that the thunderous sound of the cannons haunted him and that he feared his mother would be murdered in cold blood.

Abigail made a good reporter, describing local politics, the conditions of the camps, the health of the soldiers, and the reputations of the British generals stationed nearby. She kept John informed about their friends in Boston, many of whom wanted to leave the city. She wrote of the troubles they faced as their homes were taken over by British soldiers, and they searched in vain for meat, fish, and other provisions. Many could not escape, but some who did manage to leave found refuge with Abigail in Braintree. A few spent the night and moved on, while others stayed for a week or two.

The house was often full, the beds taken up by friends and strangers. Abigail provided meals for the refugees as she did for the colonial militiamen who passed through Braintree on the Old Coastal Road. Though she was well supplied with meat and milk, she had no coffee or sugar to offer her guests.

"I endeavored to be very insensible and heroic, yet my heart felt like a heart of lead."

–Abigail Adams, in a letter to John Adams

On May 24, 1775, Abigail wrote that the British soldiers had marched past Weymouth on their way to Grape Island. The town's women and children, along with the elderly—and most of her own family—had escaped. Her aunt fled in a cart, taking her bed with her. John's two brothers, however, remained behind to fight in the battle that followed on Grape Island. The battle was fierce, and Abigail's uncle, Dr. Cotton Tufts, stayed to care for the wounded, treating as many as 500 men.

After the Battle of Bunker Hill on June 17, Abigail wrote John that she would stay put until conditions became unsafe. If she foresaw any danger, she would take the children to his brother's house. But Abigail bravely kept her family at home and continued to write

This letter from Abigail to John tells how her heart burst when she learned of the death of their good friend Dr. Joseph Warren, a courageous soldier, a physician, and an orator. He left behind four children.

letters to John describing all she saw and heard. In July 1775, when she met General George Washington, the new leader of the Continental Army, she told John that she especially admired his dignity as well as "the modesty" that marked "every line and feature of his face."

Abigail always let John know what the children were doing—discussing their behavior, illnesses, schooling, and tutors. Several schools had closed because of the fighting so Abigail had to rely on John Thaxter, the children's tutor. She worried that they would fall behind and she shared these concerns with John. At age 10, Nabby had become a prolific letter writer and also tried to keep her father well informed.

The children loved receiving letters from their father. "You would laugh to see them all run upon the sight of a letter—like chickens for a crumb, when the hen clucks," Abigail wrote. Yet letters from John were still arriving infrequently. Abigail felt that those she did receive were often written in haste, and she longed for a greater

The Second Continental Congress appointed George Washington commander of the Continental Army.

> "But my dear child, be of good cheer; although I am absent from you for a time, it is in the way of duty."
>
> –John Adams, in a letter to his daughter Nabby

show of tenderness, as well as more detail. She begged John to write and chided him for neglecting her. She complained that she was growing anxious and reminded him of how much she treasured his letters. Abigail made practical demands as well. She asked for needles, cloth, spices, and watermelon seeds and several times requested a bundle of pins.

When John finally did write, Abigail teased him about his brevity: "The writing is very scant, but I must not grumble." Two days later, he wrote, "It gives me more pleasure than I can express, to learn that you sustain with so much fortitude the shocks and terrors of the times. You are really brave, my dear. You are a heroine . . . " Abigail replied on July 25, "It was the longest and best letter I have had; the most leisurely, and therefore the most sentimental." She promised to take back all her complaints.

In August, after four months in Philadelphia, John finally came home. But Abigail's joy at seeing him was mixed with grief—John's brother Elihu had died of dysentery. To make matters worse, John spent only three weeks in Braintree before returning

DYSENTERY
Dysentery is an infectious disease of the digestive system.

to Philadelphia. Still, it was a welcome rest. The sessions in Congress had been long and grueling.

No sooner had John left than dysentery spread throughout the Adams household. Abigail became sick and then recovered, only to nurse their son Tommy. She cleansed the house with hot vinegar to disinfect it; it was as if her home had become a hospital. Her neighbors were also suffering. So many were ill that the church had held no meetings for four weeks.

Tommy recovered, but Abigail was soon faced with more sadness: "O my bursting heart," she wrote. "My dear mother has left me . . . " Her mother, who had also been ill with dysentery, had finally succumbed to the disease. John wrote that he grieved for their children who would no longer have their grandmother to guide and care for them. "Remember a great deal of her advice and be careful to pursue it," he told them.

It was difficult for Abigail to see her father so unhappy. He missed his wife terribly and told his daughter, "Child, I see your mother, go to what part of the house I will."

Abigail would have liked John to be with her during this time, but to make the pain bearable she reminded herself of the larger purpose of their separation. Both John and Abigail shared a vision of a new and independent country and a commitment

"*My pen is always freer than my tongue.*"

–Abigail Adams, in a letter to John Adams

to making it possible. In a letter to Abigail, John wrote that he would renounce all wealth, honor, and property to obtain peace and liberty. "All these must go, and my life too, before I can surrender the right of my country to a free Constitution."

Yet there were many questions to be answered and Abigail was quick to raise them. On November 27, 1775, she wrote, "If we separate from Britain, what code of laws will be established? How shall we be governed so as to retain our liberties?" Power, "whether vested in many or a few" was "ever grasping. . . . The great fish swallow up the small." Independence had to be achieved, but Abigail recognized that great care must be given to the distribution of power.

John spent much time away from his family so that he could plan for the future of the country, for a new government, and for freedom.

As the year 1775 drew to a close, Abigail and John were together in Braintree with their four children. Although they had spent much of the year apart, they had grown closer through their letters. "My pen is always freer than my tongue," Abigail wrote. "I have written many things to you that I suppose I never could have talked."

chapter 5

"Remember the Ladies"

John wanted Abigail and the children to accompany him to Philadelphia on his return to Congress, but Abigail thought that would prove too difficult and expensive. She agreed to let him go without her. "I have been happy and unhappy," she wrote to Mercy Otis Warren. "I found his honour and reputation much dearer to me, than my own present pleasure and happiness, and I could by no means consent to his resigning at present. . . . The eyes of everyone are more particularly upon that assembly. . . . All those who act in public life have very unthankful offices."

In January 1776, John arrived in Philadelphia to find a lively debate centered on the recent publication of *Common Sense*—an anonymous attack on the monarchy and a "call to arms" for independence. John sent Abigail a copy of the pamphlet and commented that although he would like nothing better than a reconciliation with Britain, he saw "no prospect, no probability, no possibility." Abigail was charmed with *Common Sense* and thought that anyone who wished for the happiness of future generations would want to adopt its sentiments.

As usual, Abigail skillfully managed the farm as well as the family finances, making do with whatever provisions were available. She made soap from lye and ink from ashes and berries. Her daily chores occupied her from four in the morning until ten at night. And it was then, by candlelight, that she continued to find time to write John.

Cannons roared and the windows of the Adams house rattled as the Americans took Dorchester and Nook's Hill, just outside Boston. Abigail told John that British General William Howe had determined his men were no match for the Americans. He was reputed to have said, "My God, these fellows have done more work in one night than I could make my army do in three months." George Washington agreed to let General Howe remove his troops from Boston in peace if he did not set fire to the city. Abigail expected a bloody outcome but was grateful there was none.

While Congress deliberated on the future of the country, Abigail shared her thoughts on a new government.

COMMON SENSE;

ADDRESSED TO THE

INHABITANTS

OF

A M E R I C A,

On the following interesting

S U B J E C T S.

I. Of the Origin and Design of Government in general, with concise Remarks on the English Constitution.

II. Of Monarchy and Hereditary Succession.

III. Thoughts on the present State of American Affairs.

IV. Of the present Ability of America, with some miscellaneous Reflections.

Common Sense

When *Common Sense* was published anonymously in January 1776, it was rumored to have been written by John Adams. However, English immigrant Thomas Paine was later identified as the author. John Adams agreed wholeheartedly with the call for independence, but he had his own views on the form a new government should take.

Like John, she believed slavery should be abolished. She saw no sense in fighting for liberty for some while denying it to

FOMENT
To foment is to stir up or provoke.

others. She also urged John to "remember the ladies" in the new code of laws and to "be more generous and favorable to them than your ancestors." Knowing that British law gave men more rights than women, she added, "do not put such unlimited power into the hands of husbands. Remember, all men would be tyrants if they could. If particular care

British troops evacuated Boston on March 17, 1776, ending an 11-month occupation.

Abigail melted pewter and used this bullet mold to make bullets for the militia.

and attention is not paid to the ladies, we are determined to foment a rebellion, and will not hold ourselves bound by any laws in which we have no voice or representation."

John thought Abigail's ideas were presumptuous, as well as absurd, and called her "saucy." He assured Abigail that men would never exercise their full power: "In practice, you know we are the subjects: We have only the name of masters." Abigail would not let the subject rest. "I cannot say that I think you are very generous to the ladies," she wrote, "for, whilst you are proclaiming peace and good-will to men, emancipating all nations, you insist upon retaining an absolute power over wives." Women, she cautioned, had it in their power to free themselves and subdue their masters.

Abigail wrote to her friend Mercy to enlist her support: "I think I will get you to join me in a petition to congress . . . I ventured to speak a word in behalf of our sex, who are

Women, many of them wives or daughters of soldiers, often accompanied the men to the battle camp. Most cooked and tended to the wounded; a few engaged in battle.

Thoughts on Government

In March 1776, John anonymously published his response to Thomas Paine's *Common Sense*. In a work titled *Thoughts on Government,* John stated that the "happiness of society is the end of government" and he advocated an "empire of laws, and not of men." He stressed the importance of the separation of powers and outlined a structure that would include a legislative branch with two houses, a governor who would take on an executive role and be chosen annually by the legislature, and an independent judiciary. He also underscored the value of "laws for the liberal education of youth, especially of the lower class of people." He declared, "No expense for this purpose would be thought extravagant."

rather hardly dealt with by the laws of England which gives such unlimited power to the husband to use his wife ill." Ultimately, Congress did not address the issue, but Abigail and Mercy would pave the way for the women's rights advocates who came later.

Although John was not swayed by Abigail's arguments, he valued her opinions. He learned more from her than he did from the newspapers. When Abigail wrote about the need to fortify Boston and the election of representatives to the Massachusetts council, John was appreciative of her reporting skills. He read her letters again and again, and wrote, "You shine as a stateswoman of late, as well as a farmeress."

Throughout the spring the delegates debated independence and the best course of action. John Dickinson, the pacifist delegate from Pennsylvania, favored seeking a peaceful resolution. But others were more impetuous and were swayed by John Adams. By this time, John had become a respected and persuasive leader in Congress, admired for his honesty and deep convictions, a great thinker as well as a man of action. On May 10, he took the floor. His speech calling for independence from Britain would resound in the hearts and minds of all the delegates. The British would soon brand him as a traitor— a crime punishable by death.

On June 7, Richard Henry Lee from Virginia introduced a resolution declaring that the colonies had a right to be free and independent. John seconded the motion. Together with four other delegates, he formed a committee to prepare a declaration of independence. Thomas Jefferson, another delegate from Virginia, was chosen to write the document.

While the committee worked on the declaration, Abigail, at home in Braintree, worried about the smallpox epidemic that had broken out in Boston. She wanted her family to be inoculated so they could not contract the

Medical research in Abigail's time had made many advances, but procedures such as inoculations were still risky.

Slavery in the Colonies

The first Africans to come to North America arrived in Virginia in 1619. By the start of the revolution, 500,000 men, women, and children—one fifth of the population of the colonies—were slaves of African descent. The Quakers were the first to oppose slavery, but many others spoke out against it. In 1774, the colonies started to pass laws to prohibit the importation of slaves. Many people wanted the Declaration of Independence to include a condemnation of slavery.

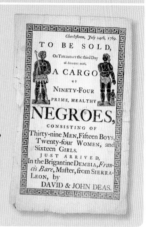

disease. At the time, the procedure was relatively new and the risks were high: permanent scarring, illness, and even death. Abigail took the children to Boston for treatment. Joining her sister Mary and her family, her sister Elizabeth, and the tutor John Thaxter, they set up housekeeping in her aunt and uncle's house. Abigail and her family did not come empty-handed, but brought along a cow, hay, and wood to be kept in the stable.

Abigail, Johnny, and Tommy recovered easily from their inoculations; Nabby and Charley did not fare as well. Nabby became quite ill, and Charley even more so. John, not knowing about the complications, was pleased to hear about the inoculations. He urged his family not to stay confined inside, but to get some fresh air.

INOCULATION

Inoculation is a medical procedure in which a patient is given a mild form of a disease to build defenses against a stronger form.

John's letter also brought news that the most important question "whichever was debated in America" had been decided: The colonies had approved the Declaration of Independence. Its intention left no ambiguity: "These United Colonies are, and of right ought to be, free and independent States." The greatness of the moment was not lost on John or Abigail.

Abigail took great pride in knowing that John had been a leader in laying the foundation for the new country. Yet she regretted that a clause to end the slave trade had not been included in the declaration. Abigail still saw no justice in proclaiming freedom for the colonists while denying it to the slaves of African descent.

On July 18, Abigail joined crowds of people

John Adams, Thomas Jefferson, and Benjamin Franklin present the Declaration of Independence to John Hancock, president of the Continental Congress. This painting by John Trumbull now hangs in the rotunda of the U.S. Capitol.

John first visited Charles Willson Peale's studio in Philadelphia in 1776. Years later the artist would paint this portrait.

to hear the Declaration read aloud from the balcony of the State House. Cheers were heard, cannons were discharged, and bells rang. The King's Arms were taken down from the statehouse in Boston. Everyone was filled with hope and joyful expectation.

Nabby, however, was still suffering from her inoculation. Abigail bravely nursed her through the ordeal. Only later did John learn that Nabby had become terribly swollen and was covered with over 600 pockmarks. When Nabby eventually recovered, the entire family underwent "purification" and all were treated with smoke to disinfect their clothing and belongings. Two months passed before the family was well enough to return home.

While Abigail oversaw the children's lessons on a daily basis, John continued to take a deep interest in their education—even from afar. He exclaimed in one letter: "Posterity! You will never know how much it cost the present generation to preserve your freedom! I hope you

will make a good use of it!" He urged Abigail to teach
the children to be brave and honest and to scorn injustice.
He wanted them to learn music at an early age, stretch
their imaginations, and develop their writing skills. He
impressed upon Johnny the importance of history and
encouraged him to study the seeds of revolution in
America and around the world.

Abigail thought schooling for girls was just as necessary,
and she was quick to point this out to John. "Your
sentiments of the importance of education in women are
exactly agreeable to my own," John replied.

When John returned to Braintree in October 1776, he
hoped to stay for good. But once again, he was elected to
Congress. Abigail hated for him to leave; still, as before, she
was willing to let him go. This time, however, he was headed
for a different city. The fighting in the north had been
intense—Fort Washington in New York had fallen. When
the British started moving south toward Philadelphia, the
delegates decided to convene in Baltimore. In January, John
left to join them; Abigail, now pregnant, feared for John's
safety so far from home, and wrote, "I feel as if you were
gone to a foreign country.
Philadelphia seemed close
by; but now I hardly know
how to reconcile myself to
the thought that you are five
hundred miles distant; but

> "I feel as if you were gone to a foreign country."
>
> –Abigail Adams, in a letter to John Adams

though distant, you are always near." John wrote to reassure her that he found the city agreeable although food and drink were expensive.

As months passed, Abigail, still in Braintree, was becoming increasingly uncomfortable with her pregnancy. One night in July, she awoke suffering from a shaking fit. She feared for the baby's health and soon went into labor. In between pains, she took up her pen to tell John how much a letter addressed to her, his "dearest friend," had meant. She gave birth the next morning, but the baby girl was stillborn. She could not bear to write her husband. John Thaxter, the children's tutor wrote to tell him of the death of the child. Abigail was despondent. She wrote John that although they had been married almost 13 years "not more than half that time have we had the happiness of living together."

Abigail took great care in seeing that not only her sons, but also her daughter, were well educated.

She regretted all the time John spent away from his children, and she worried that they had suffered from his absence.

Her thoughts then turned to the war. She was disturbed by the fighting, the blood that had been shed, and the lives that had been lost. "How my heart recoils at the idea. Why is man called humane, when he delights so much in blood, slaughter, and devastation?" In the last year, the casualties had multiplied greatly. She had not foreseen so much death and destruction.

Field Hospitals

Many of the army's sick and wounded were cared for in makeshift hospitals in or close to the army camp. Doctors used medicinal herbs and primitive surgical tools, and women volunteered as nurses. John Adams noted the lack of soap and vinegar for cleaning, as well as the scarcity of food and tents. He wrote that for every man killed in battle, 10 died of disease.

John shared Abigail's deep feelings and concerns. Visiting a burying ground in Philadelphia, he was overcome by emotion. So many had died, not only in battle but also from disease spread by the unsanitary conditions in the army camp. "Our frying-pans and gridirons slay more than the sword," he wrote.

In November 1777, Abigail and John's 11-month separation finally drew to a close, and John returned home. He had been looking forward to being back on the farm and walking through the cornfields and orchards with his children by his side. Abigail wanted nothing more.

chapter **6**

On Her Own

In February 1778, Abigail again said good-bye to her husband. This time, John was braving the seas to cross the Atlantic. Congress was sending him to Paris to help negotiate an alliance with France in war against Britain. Abigail had not wanted him to accept the appointment, and John had offered to refuse it. But Abigail knew France's help was key to America achieving its independence. In the end, though they felt conflicted, they decided John should go. He would take with him their oldest son John Quincy, who was now 10 years old.

The sea was choppy, the wind was strong, and the country was at war. A winter ocean voyage was dangerous, and few would undertake such a journey during wartime. Abigail knew John was putting himself and their son

Benjamin Franklin was famous for his writings and inventions, his humor and curiosity, as well as his wise sayings.

at risk the moment they set foot on the ship. What Abigail did not know was just how great the risk would be. John's ship, the *Boston*, a vessel armed with 24 guns, was caught in terrible storms and later had a perilous encounter. Sailing toward what he thought was a British merchant ship, Captain Samuel Tucker told John to go below. John refused and stayed on deck. Unfortunately, the British vessel was actually a warship! Gunfire was exchanged and the *Boston*

John gave this locket to Abigail in 1778 before he set sail for France. A lock of John's hair is preserved inside.

escaped unharmed. Still, it had been a close call.

Father and son docked at the French port of Bordeaux, then traveled by land to Paris. There, they met with Benjamin Franklin, the American author, scientist, and diplomat, who had also been appointed to participate in the negotiations. But no sooner had John arrived than he learned that his mission had already been accomplished. The French government, swayed by the American victory at the Battle of Saratoga, had finally agreed to an alliance.

Several of John's letters to Abigail were lost at sea, so it was several months before Abigail received word that her husband and son had arrived safely. When she did, she replied that she wished she could be with them but would have to be consoled by tales of their adventures. She told

John Quincy how difficult it was to part with him and urged him to acquire useful knowledge, but

The grand palace of Versailles, with its magnificent gardens and fountains, was home to Louis XVI and Marie Antoinette.

cautioned, "Great learning and superior abilities will be of little value and small estimation, unless virtue, honor, truth, and integrity are added to them."

John and his son both studied the French language and immersed themselves in French culture. They enjoyed the company of Ben Franklin in Paris. The older statesman entertained John and his son with his wit and charm and introduced them to his French friends. John was amused and intrigued by the fine food, exotic manners, fancy clothes, elaborate theater, sophisticated

"Nature and art have conspired to render everything here delightful."

–John Adams, in a letter to Abigail Adams

conversation, and displays of wealth. On May 8, 1778, he donned a new elegant outfit, complete with sword, and was presented to King Louis XVI at the palace at Versailles. He would meet Queen Marie Antoinette at dinner. "Nature and art have conspired to render everything here delightful," he wrote in a letter to Abigail. "There are no people in the world who take so much pains to please."

Abigail was enjoying no such pleasures. Winter in Braintree was colder than ever. "By the mountains of snow which surround me, I could almost fancy myself in Greenland," Abigail wrote. She was housebound with her two sons while Nabby was in Plymouth visiting friends. "How lonely are my days! How solitary are my nights!" she exclaimed. Months passed without her hearing from her son or her husband. She longed for John to tell her more about Europe; John, on

Louis XVI and Marie Antoinette

In 1770, at the age of 15, Louis-Auguste, heir to the French throne, married Marie Antoinette, the 14-year-old daughter of the archduchess of Austria and the Holy Roman Emperor. Louis and Marie Antoinette ruled France from 1774 to 1792. Beloved at first, the king and queen were later condemned for their extravagances, and were executed by revolutionaries in 1793.

John completed the Massachusetts Constitution in October 1779. It is the oldest written constitution still in use today.

the other hand, was reluctant to divulge too much, fearing that his letters would be intercepted by spies. Although he revealed little about the political situation, he showed his usual concern for the children. He urged Nabby to study her French, reminding her to transcribe passages, conjugate verbs, and practice every day.

Benjamin Franklin had been named minister to the court of Louis XVI, and in May 1779 John was told he was no longer needed in Paris. John resented not having been chosen as minister, but he also longed to be home. As he and his son prepared for their departure, John reflected on all the progress his son had made in French and the marvelous experiences they had shared in seeing a new country. He was proud of his son for adjusting well and always maintaining his good humor.

John and John Quincy sailed home on the *Sensible* and arrived on August 2, taking Abigail by surprise. The separation had been difficult because there was so little

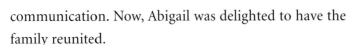

communication. Now, Abigail was delighted to have the family reunited.

John quickly took on a new task—he was asked to write the Massachusetts Constitution. It would be a significant document, later to be used as a model for the United States Constitution. It included both a declaration of rights and an outline of the structure of the government.

Sadly, Abigail and John's time together was only temporary. Within months, John was asked to return to Europe. Congress wanted him to be ready to negotiate a peace treaty with Great Britain should the need arise. Once again, he would sail to Europe; this time he would be accompanied by John Quincy and Charles, as well as John Thaxter, the boys' former tutor and John's new private secretary. When the party set sail on November 15, 1779, Abigail was distraught, knowing she would be separated from John and two of her children for months, if not years. She worried most about Charles, who was only nine years old.

The Constitution of Massachusetts

John Adams modeled the Massachusetts Constitution after the ideas in his *Thoughts on Government.* He proposed a separation of powers and a system of checks and balances, similar to those later included in the U.S. Constitution. The government would consist of a legislative branch (with both a senate and a house of representatives), an executive branch (the governor's office), and a judiciary power. The document also assured the continued survival of Harvard College and encouraged the advancement of literature.

It was not until the end of February that Abigail learned that their ship had arrived not in France, but in Spain. A leak had forced an early landing. John and his companions found they had to cross mountains by mule and on foot. They traveled 1,000 miles (1,609 km) across bad roads before arriving in Paris. By this point, Abigail was resigned to enduring long stretches without word from John. And again, she knew nothing of the dangers he was facing until they were over.

Once in Paris, John concerned himself with the boys' schooling. "I must study politics and war, that my sons may have liberty to study mathematics and philosophy," he wrote to Abigail. "My sons ought to study mathematics and philosophy, geography, natural history and naval architecture . . . in order to give their children a right to study painting, poetry, music, architecture. . . . "

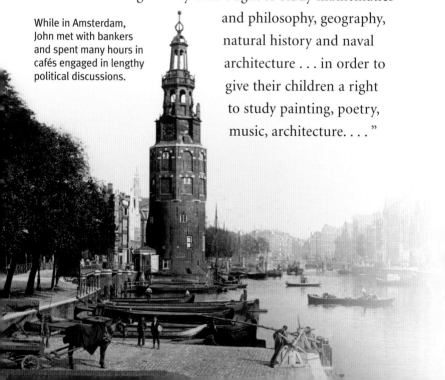

While in Amsterdam, John met with bankers and spent many hours in cafés engaged in lengthy political discussions.

John was pleased to have the company of his sons and Abigail was always delighted to receive news from her far-flung family. "Charles is as well beloved here as at home," John wrote. "Wherever he goes everybody loves him." Later that year, Abigail learned that John and the boys had gone to Amsterdam so that John could secure a loan from the Netherlands. The boys were sent to school in Leiden, 29 miles (47 km) from the city,

Young John Quincy studied Latin at the insistence of his father, who also wanted to prepare him for a career in public service.

where they studied the classics. But Abigail heard little from them—and she sorely missed them.

Abigail often suffered from bouts of illness and exhaustion. When she grew agitated, she had to take to her bed. She also developed rheumatism, an inflammation in her joints that was quite painful. Still, she continued to look after the farm and even bought more

"I must study politics and war, that my sons may have liberty to study mathematics and philosophy."

–John Adams, in a letter to Abigail Adams

land. (Since women could not own property, she bought the land in John's name.) Abigail now had a total of 108 acres to manage. With two children gone she also had more time to take on a new venture. She asked John to send tea, cloth, ribbons, and handkerchiefs and made plans to sell the items in Massachusetts. John also sent blue Canton dishes imported from China, some to keep and some to sell. Although she only made a small profit, the income made a difference. Abigail suggested to John that they purchase a retreat in the woods of Vermont where they could find "peace and domestic happiness" and retire from "the vexations, toils, and hazards of public life."

In the summer of 1781, Francis Dana, an American from Massachusetts who had accompanied John Adams to Paris as his secretary, was named minister to the court of Catherine the Great, the Russian empress. Francis asked John Quincy to travel with him as his translator. (John Quincy spoke French, the official language of the court, but Francis did not.) John, who wanted his son to see the world and experience new adventures, agreed to let him go.

Charles became homesick without his brother and asked to return to Braintree. John sent him off with two American friends. Their ship left the Netherlands but did not have enough supplies to cross the ocean, and returned to Europe, docking in Spain. The American friends arranged for passage on a different ship, and the group set sail again, bound for Massachusetts.

John had made the decision to let both boys depart on their journeys without consulting Abigail. The mail was slow and unreliable, making communication difficult. In September, Abigail heard that Charles was on his way home. Knowing he had first left Amsterdam in August, she expected him to appear at any moment. For months, she heard nothing. She wished John had asked her advice before letting him return. The waiting became unbearable and made her anxious. She worried constantly throughout the fall and winter. Then, on January 21, 1782, five months after he had left Amsterdam, Charles arrived—and Abigail's spirits soared. The boy she had not seen for more than two years was home.

Upon arrival in America, Charles heard the good news: The British had surrendered at

John Trumbull's *The Surrender of Lord Cornwallis at Yorktown* now hangs in the Rotunda of the U.S. Capitol.

Yorktown on October 19, 1781. The war was over, and Americans had won their independence. But when word reached John in Europe, he knew there was still much work to be done. It would take more than a year to negotiate a treaty with Britain. Meanwhile, he continued to seek aid from the Dutch. The following April, the Netherlands recognized American independence and, within months, John had negotiated a treaty of commerce with the Dutch republic. He also secured a sorely needed loan of two million dollars.

Time passed and still John did not return to Massachusetts. On November 13, 1782, Abigail wrote, "I have lived to see the close of the third year of our separation. . . . Life is too short to have the dearest of its enjoyments curtailed." Abigail and Nabby proposed coming to meet John in Europe, but John worried about their safety. To Nabby he wrote, "I have too much tenderness for you, my dear child, to permit you to cross the Atlantic." He continued to take a keen interest in her education and, as he had with John Quincy, he encouraged her to study history, "which is as entertaining and instructive to the female as to the male sex. My advice to you would be to read the history of your own country."

> *"Whether there should be peace or war, I shall come home in the summer."*
>
> –John Adams, in a letter to Abigail Adams

John planned to return home and wrote to Congress that he wished to resign. In December, John wrote Abigail, "Whether there should be peace or war, I shall come home in the summer." Two months later, on February 18, 1783, he wrote, "I am determined not to wait for an acceptance of my resignation. Don't think, therefore of coming to Europe. If you do, we shall cross each other, and I shall arrive in America about the same time that you may arrive

John Adams, Benjamin Franklin, and John Jay signed the Treaty of Paris. This treaty recognized the 13 colonies as free and independent states.

in Europe." He finished with these words: "You have nothing to do but wait to receive your old friend."

Yet before long, he would have a change of heart. On September 3, 1783, John Adams, Benjamin Franklin, and John Jay, a former delegate to the Continental Congress, signed the long-awaited Treaty of Paris, bringing the American Revolution to a formal conclusion. John was asked to stay in Paris to negotiate a treaty of commerce with Britain. He would not return home. If Abigail wanted to see him, she would have to cross the Atlantic.

chapter 7

Crossing the Atlantic

Although a summer voyage was safer than a winter one, it was not without risk. Abigail mustered her courage to brave the ocean, but it was difficult to leave family and friends. It could be years before she would return. John's mother thought she was seeing her daughter-in-law for the last time, and "tears rolled down her aged cheek."

Ocean Voyages

Transatlantic voyages were long, dangerous, and often unpleasant undertakings. Capture by pirates or enemy ships, attacks at sea, and violent storms were not unheard of. More common was debilitating seasickness— experienced by both Abigail and Nabby aboard the Active. The smell of the ship, indigestion caused by old or too-salty food, and the motion of tossing of the ship over the waves often made passengers miserable. Quarters were usually cramped—Abigail and Nabby's cabin was only eight feet (2.5 meters) square, with a single small, grated window. So as not to suffocate they kept the door open and closed it only to dress. When the ship's cargo of oil started to leak, they became even more nauseated. "You who have never tried the sea can form no idea of it," Abigail wrote.

Charles and Tommy would stay behind with Abigail's sister Elizabeth in Haverhill, Massachusetts. Elizabeth's husband, John Shaw, was a minister and scholar who would tutor them in Greek and Latin. Abigail dreaded saying good-bye to her sons; knowing Nabby would accompany her made it bearable. And she was pleased that Nabby would be distancing herself from her suitor, Royall Tyler, a young lawyer in Braintree. Abigail didn't think much of him—in her view he was neither serious nor ambitious. Abigail and John agreed that a separation between the two would serve them well, and that the trip to Europe would give them time to test the relationship.

Abigail and Nabby packed several trunks with clothes, dishes, and books. They also brought a cow aboard the ship to provide milk during the voyage. The *Active* departed on a warm June day, but no sooner had the ship set sail than mother and daughter both became terribly seasick. The lack of cleanliness didn't help, and the dampness of the ship made Abigail's rheumatism worse. The food was not to her liking either, so Abigail made arrangements to lend a hand to the cook, making various desserts (or "puddings" as she called them). Still, she felt so terrible that she wrote, "I am more and more of the mind that a Lady ought not to go to sea."

On July 20, after 30 days at sea, the *Active* docked at the English port of Deal. Abigail and Nabby went overland by stagecoach to London, arriving the following day. They found a room at a hotel in Covent Garden, in the center of the city,

At the end of a 30-day voyage, Abigail and Nabby disembarked at Deal on the British coast. near its largest market and not far from the king's palace. John was detained at the Hague, in the Netherlands, on a diplomatic mission and sent John Quincy to meet them. John planned to have his son bring Abigail and Nabby back to the Netherlands, but he was so anxious to see them that he abruptly changed his plans.

Nabby recalled returning to the hotel one afternoon: "When I entered, I saw upon the table a hat with two books in it; everything around appeared altered, without my knowing in what particular." She asked Esther, a servant, "Has mamma received letters that have determined her departure? When does she go? Whose hat is that in the other room! Whose trunk is this? Whose sword and cane?" Nabby did not wait for Esther to answer. "It is my father's," she said. "Where is he?"

Esther replied, "In the room above." Nabby described the scene that followed: "Up I flew, and to his chamber, where he was lying down. He raised himself upon my knocking softly

at the door, and received me with all the tenderness of an affectionate parent after so long an absence." After being separated for four-and-a-half years, Abigail, Nabby, and John were now reunited.

> "[He] received me with all the tenderness of an affectionate parent after so long an absence."
>
> –Abigail "Nabby" Adams

John wanted Abigail and Nabby to see the sites—the British Museum, Westminster Abbey, and St. Paul's Church. He encouraged Nabby to keep a journal of her trip: "I need not say to you that the end of travel, as well as study, is not the simple gratification of curiosity, or to enable one to shine in conversation, but to make us wiser and better."

The Adams family spent three weeks in London and then departed, traveling over a mountainous road to the coast. Eventually, they crossed the channel by

Covent Garden was noted for its bustling open-air market and lively outdoor entertainment.

The Adams family lived in this grand residence in Auteuil from August 1784 to May 1785.

boat and went by carriage through the French countryside to Paris. They settled into a magnificent house in Auteuil, a town on the outskirts of Paris. The house was quite grand—with three stories and more than 50 rooms, most of them small, but a few large enough to receive company, and one paneled with mirrors. The spacious grounds boasted five acres of orange trees, a fish pond, and a romantic garden.

Abigail and Nabby were dazzled by their new surroundings and intrigued by the French people, fashion, and customs. Abigail had to adjust to a dramatic change. She no longer spent her evenings alone writing letters; now she hosted dinner parties for 20. She went regularly to the theater and the opera. The family was entertained by Benjamin

Thomas Jefferson served as minister to France from 1784 to 1789.

Franklin and became close friends with Thomas Jefferson. Thomas had lost his wife before coming to Paris and he relished time with both Abigail and John. They saw each other frequently and discussed their children, as well as politics, theater, and the leading opera stars. Thomas joined the Adamses for meals and took a special interest in John Quincy. And when Thomas learned that his two-year-old daughter, Lucy, had died of whooping cough, Abigail and John were there to comfort him.

Much of what the Adamses did was enjoyable. They viewed paintings by Raphael and Michelangelo at the Palais Royal, a palace once home to the king. They took long walks through the Bois de Boulogne, a huge park with forests and meadows.

Parisians gather in the Tuileries to watch in astonishment as a hot-air balloon rises above the clouds.

During a visit to the Tuileries gardens they watched as a hot-air balloon rose into the air—a new technology at the time. The day after Queen Marie Antoinette gave birth to the long-awaited prince, they attended a memorable service at Notre Dame Cathedral in Paris to give thanks for his birth.

Abigail and Nabby also witnessed other aspects of city life. They discovered the Enfants Trouvés—an orphanage for abandoned babies, run by the Charity Sisters, a religious order of nuns. Inside there were more than 100 cradles; in one year, the Charity Sisters had taken in 6,000 children. Later Abigail and Nabby

While in Paris Abigail enjoyed watching plays by Molière. Both a playwright and an actor, Molière cleverly satirized French society. Greed and hypocrisy were among his favorite topics.

visited the convent school that Thomas Jefferson's daughter attended. There, they watched a ceremony in which several young women, with wreaths of flowers on their heads, took vows to become nuns.

Abigail also saw much that made her uncomfortable. The vast wealth and splendor were overwhelming. So many of the French people she met reveled in frivolity—they loved parties, good food, and wine. Yet, as the daughter of a minister, accustomed to a simpler lifestyle, she was often appalled.

Paris Opera

The Adamses spent many delightful evenings at the opera and the theater. Abigail was enchanted by the sumptuous costumes, the lavish scenery, and the splendor of the theaters. Especially popular were works by Wolfgang Amadeus Mozart, Jean-Baptiste Lully, considered the founder of French opera, and Christoph Gluck, a composer who had been commissioned by Marie Antoinette to write several new operas.

On April 26, 1785, John received a letter naming him minister to the Court of St. James's in London. He and Abigail would take Nabby with them to London, but they had other plans for John Quincy. They both wanted him to return to America to attend college.

John Quincy had received an excellent education in France and the Netherlands. He had traveled to

St. Petersburg and throughout Europe. He had been taught
by tutors and by both his parents. He spoke perfect French
and had studied Latin, English literature, history, and
mathematics. But he would still have to be tutored in
Greek before he could be accepted to Harvard. He would
return to Boston to study with his uncle—a minister,
teacher, and Greek scholar. As he boarded the ship on May
12, 1785, John Quincy was given a special mission: The
Marquis de Lafayette, a well-known Frenchman who had
fought in the American Revolution, asked him to care for
seven dogs that were being shipped to America as a gift
for George Washington. The dogs were welcome company
on the long voyage.

A week later, Abigail, John,
and Nabby left Auteuil by carriage.
Abigail would miss the garden

When Abigail and John
first arrived in London they
rented temporary rooms at
the Bath Hotel in Piccadilly,
a fashionable area close to
St. James's Palace.

John Quincy helped transport seven French hounds to America, a gift to George Washington from the Marquis de Lafayette. Washington raised and bred the hounds at his home in Mount Vernon.

at Auteuil and Thomas Jefferson's company. But once again, she was poised for a new adventure.

Nabby and her parents arrived in London on May 26. They had entertained each other during the journey by reading aloud from Thomas Jefferson's recently published book, *Notes on the State of Virginia*—a history of Jefferson's home state and a present from the author. The Adamses rented temporary rooms at the Bath Hotel in Piccadilly, a fashionable neighborhood of London, while they looked for more permanent lodging. Within weeks they had found a pleasant house on Grosvenor Square, overlooking a lovely park. On June 9, John signed a lease for 21 months. The family unpacked their clothes and books, arranged and rearranged their furnishings, and readied the house for guests.

Soon they would be comfortably settled in the land that had once been home to their ancestors. Abigail needed no reminding that it was also the country from which Americans had recently won their independence. Less than two years had passed since John had put his signature on the peace treaty. It now fell to John and to her to reach out in friendship to those once considered enemies.

chapter **8**

Call to London

John's first public duty was to meet King George III at St. James's Palace. He prepared with some trepidation, remembering that during the Revolutionary War he had been branded a traitor by the British. On June 1, 1785, he dressed with care and was presented to the king. Both men were moved by the significance of the moment. "Sir, your words have been so proper, upon this occasion, that I cannot but say I am gratified that you are the man chosen to be the Minister," King George concluded at the end of the visit.

Before long, Abigail and Nabby were also introduced to the royal family. It took mother and daughter the entire morning to dress and fix their hair. They arrived at the palace and were instructed to wait in line. Four hours passed. Abigail was dismayed at the delay, but when her turn came to meet the king she was charmed.

King George III welcomes John Adams to St. James's Palace on June 1, 1785.

While Nabby was in France, she and Royall Tyler had corresponded regularly with each other and exchanged miniature portraits. But as the months passed, letters from Royall arrived less frequently. Nabby worried that he was losing interest in her. After her family moved to London, Nabby—her pride wounded—ended the relationship and returned Royall's letters and portrait. She wanted Royall to return her letters and portrait to her aunt in Braintree, but Royall did not follow through, telling Nabby's aunt that he hoped to win her back by coming to London.

However, Nabby now found herself thinking less and less of Royall Tyler. There was another young man who had caught her fancy: Colonel William Stephens Smith, the handsome secretary to the American legation in London. William was the son of a New York merchant. After graduating from Princeton College in 1774, he had studied law. During the revolution, he became an officer in the Continental Army and had served under General Washington. Now that he was in London working with her father, Nabby saw quite a bit of him.

Abigail did not think it was proper for Nabby to become involved with one gentleman immediately after breaking off a romance with another. Aware of Abigail's feelings, William left abruptly on a European tour. When he returned several months later, he wrote a formal request to Abigail asking to marry her daughter. Both John and Abigail were delighted and wholeheartedly approved of William. The engagement

Nabby was 19-years old when Mather Brown painted this formal portrait of her.

was a happy one, and lasted six months. Finally, William and Nabby were married at the Adams home on June 11, 1786. It was a small wedding with very few guests.

With John gone for long stretches of time, Abigail had grown quite close to Nabby, her only daughter. Nabby had always helped her mother with the chores and, while the boys had traveled with John or studied away from home, Nabby had remained with Abigail and become her confidante. Although Abigail was quite fond of her new son-in-law and pleased with the match, she also felt a sense of loss. Her relationship with her daughter would never be the same. Nabby and William would want to lead their own lives.

While in London, Abigail and John met other Americans, including the architect Charles Bulfinch, as well as several painters: Benjamin West, John Trumbull, Mather Brown, and John Singleton Copley. They also saw the great actress Sarah Siddons perform in *Macbeth* and *Othello* and attended a performance of Handel's *Messiah* at Westminster Abbey.

The Adamses also kept up a correspondence with their good friend Thomas Jefferson. John and Thomas exchanged views on politics and diplomacy; Abigail and Thomas exchanged wish lists. She requested French shoes, lace, and dessert plates while Thomas asked for a dozen English shirts, a tablecloth, and napkins.

In March 1786, Jefferson came to London to visit his friends and negotiate a trade treaty. Once again the three enjoyed each other's company. Thomas rented rooms close by. Abigail and John entertained him at their home on Grosvenor Square and introduced him to their friends, even arranging to take him to the Court of St. James's to present him to the king.

During this time, John, Abigail, and Nabby, as well as Thomas Jefferson, had their portraits painted by Mather Brown, an artist born in Boston and living in London. John and Thomas had copies made of theirs and exchanged them as a token of friendship. In April, the two men visited many stately homes and gardens throughout England, traveling to Surrey, Reading,

Mather Brown

Mather Brown was born in 1761 in Boston. At the age of 12, he studied painting with the famous portraitist Gilbert Stuart. After moving to London, he enrolled in classes at the Royal Academy and trained in the studio of Benjamin West, another American-born painter. John Adams was fond of Brown's work and invited the artist to his home to paint the family's portraits. During his lifetime, Brown never achieved the fame to which he aspired; he died impoverished in 1831.

Stowe, and Stratford-upon-Avon. Abigail joined them to visit two great houses outside London: Osterley Park, which they found ostentatious; and Syon House, which had a beautiful gate designed by Robert Adam. Thomas spent six weeks with the Adamses before returning to Paris—it was a time that they all cherished and one that strengthened their friendship.

Abigail also traveled with John to the Netherlands, where he was sent to sign a commercial treaty with Prussia that he and Thomas Jefferson had worked hard to procure. The sea was so rough that Abigail once again suffered from seasickness—as did most of the passengers on the boat. But as soon as they landed, Abigail immediately fell in love with the country. They spent five weeks in the Netherlands and visited the major cities: the Hague, Rotterdam, Delft, Leiden, Amsterdam, and Utrecht. The land was green and fertile, the cities were clean, and the people were honest and lacked pretention. Abigail admired the simplicity of Dutch dress, but did

The three Americans—Abigail, John, and Thomas Jefferson—visited the Osterley Park mansion outside London.

Abigail and John enjoyed their time together in Amsterdam. Abigail noted the cleanliness and lack of poverty.

notice that gold earrings and bracelets were quite popular. From Amsterdam she wrote Nabby, "If politeness and attention could render a place agreeable, I have had more reason to be pleased with this country than any other I have visited." She appreciated the show of respect for heroes and patriots in paintings and sculptures. Most impressive was the statue of William I, Prince of Orange, the 16th-century Dutch hero and leader in the independence movement from Spain.

The following year brought a new addition to the Adams family. After their wedding, Nabby and William Smith had moved to their own house on Wimpole Street, but in March 1787, they returned to Grosvenor Square. Nabby, who was pregnant, wanted to have the baby in her parents' home and also looked forward to having their help. On April 2, Dr. John Jeffries, a loyalist who had left Boston during the revolution, delivered William Steuben Smith. Nabby and William were proud parents. Abigail and John, the doting grandparents, could not have been more delighted to have their first grandson under their roof.

LOYALIST
A loyalist remained loyal to Britain before and during the American Revolution.

Mather Brown painted this portrait of Colonel William Stephens Smith, secretary to the American legation—and Nabby's husband.

In June, Thomas Jefferson's eight-year-old daughter, Polly, arrived in London after five weeks at sea. She was "rough as a sailor" and angry with her father for not coming to London to meet her. Abigail took Polly and Sally Hemings, the young slave who had accompanied her, under her wing. After two days with Abigail, Polly became "the favorite of every creature in the house." Abigail bought her new clothes and books. She wrote to Thomas, "Books are her delight, and I have furnished her out a little library, and she reads to me by the hour with great distinctness, and comments on what she reads." When Thomas asked that she send his daughter to him, she replied that she did not have "the heart to force her into a carriage against her will." But in the end, she did as he requested and Polly left in tears. Abigail would always remember the young

"Now I have learnt to love you, why will they tear me from you?"

—Polly Jefferson

girl's parting words:
"O! now I have learnt to love you, why will they tear me from you?"

When the new baby was less than four months old, the Adamses and the Smiths set out by coach on a tour of England, accompanied by a nursery maid, a servant, and a footman. Abigail had not been well, and Dr. Jeffries thought the trip would do her good. They traveled for one month and covered 600 miles (965 km). They visited the cathedral in Winchester, once home

Magna Carta

Issued in 1215, the Magna Carta was one of the first legal documents to put limits on the power of the English king and to establish the rights of the people. It became a model for the U.S. Constitution.

Abigail enjoyed touring many of England's most famous cities, including Bath, shown here.

to Abigail's ancestor, Saer de Quincy, Earl of Winchester, one of the signers of the Magna Carta. They dined with friends and relatives of Abigail's brother-in-law Richard Cranch, and toured Blenheim Palace, the grand home of John Churchill, Duke of Marlborough. At Oxford University, they stopped to visit the Picture Gallery and the famous Bodleian Library with its medieval manuscripts. Near the city of Southampton, Abigail took her first dip in the sea.

These travels were exciting but also exhausting. After three years abroad, John and Abigail were ready to go back to America. At the end of the year, Congress finally voted to approve John's return home, extending its thanks to him for his service to his country. Delighted at the news, the Adamses packed their clothes, books, furniture, and china for shipping. They would take with them French chairs, their four-poster bed, a settee and a chest from the Netherlands, as well as an English rosebush.

Nabby, William, and their son were also returning to the United States and planned to settle in New York. Sorry to see her grandson leave, Abigail wrote to Nabby, "I don't like the idea that he will quite forget me. We want him here very much to enliven the scene." Nabby's departure was also hard on Abigail. In a letter to Margaret Smith, William's mother, Abigail wrote, "I have no other daughter to supply her place—but I have the satisfaction and pleasure of knowing that she has one of

SETTEE

A settee is a small sofa, often with high legs, that was popular in the 18th century.

the kindest and tenderest of husbands." In the same letter, she described Nabby as reserved, "a silent character, and in that respect very unlike her mamma."

"I have seen enough of the world, small as it has been."

–Abigail Adams

Abigail and John left London on March 30, 1788, and set out for Cowes, a port on the coast where they would await their ship. They were given a small room at the Fountain Inn. Feeling cramped, Abigail asked for better accommodations— and was relieved to find that their new room not only was larger but had a beautiful view. The Adamses departed on the *Lucretia* on April 20. However, a gale of wind forced them back into the harbor, where they remained for seven days before again setting sail.

Abigail was less seasick than she had been on her first crossing, and she enjoyed the company of the other passengers. Yet she wrote in a letter to Nabby, "I hope and pray, I may never again be left to go to sea: of all places, it is the most disagreeable, such a sameness, and such a tossing to and fro."

In her diary, she added these words: "Indeed I have seen enough of the world, small as it has been, and shall be content to learn what is further to be known from the page of history. I do not think the four years I have passed abroad the pleasantest part of my life." Abigail Adams had traveled the world, but now it was time to go home.

chapter **9**

Grand Welcome

As the *Lucretia* pulled into Boston Harbor on June 17, 1788, several thousand people gathered on the pier to welcome John and Abigail. Cannons boomed and loud cheers echoed across the water. Governor John Hancock sent a carriage to bring the Adamses back to his home on Beacon Hill. Church bells rang throughout the day and into the night.

Abigail and John were overwhelmed by their reception. Most of all, they were pleased to see their sons—Thomas was now 15, and Charles was now 18. Four years had passed since

This watercolor, painted by E. Malcolm, shows the Adamses' home as it appeared in 1798.

Abigail had last seen the boys, and now they were almost grown. Abigail's sister and brother-in-law had taken excellent care of them, but she had missed them terribly, all the same.

John Quincy was living in Newburyport, Massachusetts, when his parents arrived. He was anxious to see them, but had trouble procuring transportation. Three days later, he arrived in

Charles Adams had grown into a young man since his parents had last seen him.

Boston and met his mother at the Governor's House. (John had already gone ahead to Braintree.) Abigail and John Quincy had a joyful reunion and then traveled together to Braintree to join John.

While in Europe, John and Abigail had purchased a new house in Braintree, as well as 75 acres of fields and orchards, for the sum of £600. The new house, which became known as Peacefield, was bigger than the one they had shared when they were first married, but not as large as their houses in Europe, and at first the adjustment was difficult. Abigail wrote Nabby that she was "sadly disappointed" with the house. It was smaller than she'd expected and felt like a birdhouse.

Nevertheless, both husband and wife were happy to be back home with friends and family. John wrote approvingly

Peacefield

Although Abigail and John's new home would always be drafty in the winter, it was elegant and charming. Abigail employed numerous carpenters and masons to make renovations. She added windows to the parlor and painted the mahogany paneling white to lighten the room. She also planted daffodils, roses, and lilacs in the garden, built a small pond for the cows, and installed outdoor clotheslines for drying the laundry.

of his sons to Nabby, commending John Quincy for his fine conduct and morals and Thomas for liking "a spice of fun." He added that Charles "wins the hearts, as usual, and is the most of a gentleman of them all."

No sooner had John returned than he was elected a Massachusetts delegate to the U.S. Congress. But his political future was uncertain with the country's first presidential election only a few months away. George Washington was expected to be elected president and it was widely rumored that John would become vice president. Unlike today, presidential candidates did not have "running mates" who became their vice president if they were elected. Instead, the candidate who came in second place became vice president. Although voting started in December 1788, the final results would not be known until the following spring.

Abigail followed the political developments closely, but, as always, much of her attention was devoted to her family's needs. In November she traveled to New York to be with Nabby, who had just given birth to her second boy, named John after his grandfather.

At the end of March, the results of the election were clear: George Washington had received 69 votes. John Adams, who had received

George Washington was sworn in as the first president of the United States on April 30, 1789, at Federal Hall in New York City.

34 votes, would become vice president. Accompanied by a cavalcade, John left Massachusetts to head for the capital in New York. Everywhere he went, people came out to cheer.

Abigail did not attend Washington's inauguration, but stayed in Braintree to finish fixing up the new home. She told John she would not come to New York until they had a place to live. Eager for her to come, John found a beautiful house named Richmond Hill, overlooking the North River (now called the Hudson), with views of New Jersey and Long Island.

INAUGURATION

During an inauguration ceremony, the president is formally installed in office.

Abigail had just unpacked the last crate in the Braintree house and now had to start repacking. She organized the move and once again said her good-byes. This time, her niece Louisa Smith (her brother William's daughter) accompanied her. When Abigail reached New York, she was pleasantly surprised. The house and garden, with a gravel walk and a beautiful row of trees, were lovely.

As First Lady, Martha Washington was an unassuming hostess. She also doted on her grandchildren.

As wife of the vice president, Abigail spent much of her time entertaining, often assisting first lady Martha Washington with receptions. The two women offered their guests lemonade and a new delicacy gaining in popularity—ice cream. Abigail also held open houses on Mondays and gave numerous dinner parties for the senators and their families. Happily, she had a housekeeper, a cook, a footman, a steward, and a housemaid to help.

Both John and Abigail enjoyed George and Martha Washington's company. The two couples frequently dined together and attended the theater. After an evening out, Abigail wrote her sister, "I found myself much more deeply impressed than I ever did before their Majesties of Britain." What appealed to her most was that the Washingtons did not seem pretentious. The president was both dignified and likable, and Martha "unassuming" and "unaffected." She was also "dotingly fond of her grandchildren, to whom she is quite the Grandmamma."

Not all of Abigail's time was taken up with dinners and official obligations. Her children were young adults now, but she still worried about them. Thomas had grown thin and pale, and Charles was too fat. She also took a keen interest in her grandchildren. Although she lavished attention on them, she was not one to spoil them, nor did she hesitate to pass on advice. When she learned that her sister had become a grandmother, she wrote, "Can you really

At the time of Washington's inauguration, it was still unclear how a U.S. president should be addressed. Abigail and John favored "His Excellency," but the less formal "Mr. President" won out.

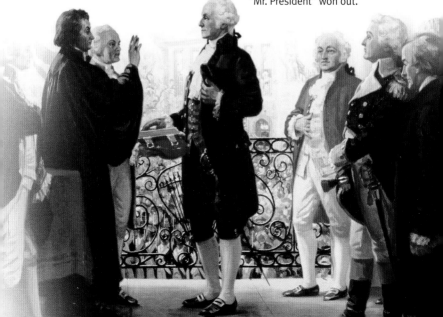

The paths along the Schuylkill River featured trees beside the docks. However, the trees in front of the Adams house had been cut down by the British.

believe that you are a Grandmamma? Does not the little fellow feel as if he was really your own?"

In the fall of 1790, Philadelphia was made the new capital of the nation. Abigail had no desire to leave New York and was not looking forward to another move. "I feel low spirited and heartless," she wrote to her sister. "I am going amongst another new set of company, to form new acquaintances, to make and receive a hundred ceremonious visits, not one of ten from which I shall derive any pleasure or satisfaction."

Abigail had always hated having her family scattered; at least in New York she was close to Nabby, William, and the children. But she had no family in Philadelphia. "My separation from Mrs. Smith [Nabby] is painful to me on many accounts," she wrote.

In November 1790, John and Abigail moved to a large brick house in Bush Hill, just outside Philadelphia, overlooking the Schuylkill River. The grove and gravel walk in the back were quite beautiful, but Abigail had little time to enjoy the outdoors. She was busy caring for her grandson, Johnny, while Nabby's husband, William, was in England on business. Abigail also had to nurse her son Thomas who was suffering from a severe case of rheumatism—he had lost the use of his arms and legs. Thomas's health improved by the new year, but Abigail was still concerned about the fact that Nabby was alone in New York. Her husband was not expected back for several months.

During the summer, Abigail and John escaped to Braintree. There, life was less hectic, and they could spend time with old friends. In May 1791, on their way north from Philadelphia, they stopped in New York to see Nabby and enjoyed a wonderful reunion. But the following year William announced that his business would again take him to Europe, this time for a two-year stint. Nabby and the children would accompany him. "This you may be sure is a heavy stroke to me," Abigail wrote to her sister Mary.

The unwelcome news may have contributed to Abigail's poor health. She soon became very ill and was bedridden for six weeks, suffering from what was called "intermittent fever," now known as malaria, a disease spread by mosquitoes. In her letter to Mary, she added, "Indeed my dear Sister it is very hard to part with my only daughter. It has

Nabby and her family remained close to her mother's heart and mind, despite the distance that was often between them.

depressed my spirits very much through my sickness, but we must all have our trials, some of one kind and some of another."

Both George Washington and John Adams were elected to a second term in 1792. But this time, Abigail would stay at Peacefield—which was now part of the newly incorporated city of Quincy, Massachusetts, named after Abigail's grandfather. The strain of going back and forth had proved too much for her. She had never fully recovered from her illness, and was still prone to rheumatism. One remedy she tried involved drawing blood, a procedure that may have made her condition worse. Another reason to remain in Quincy was that the expense of running two houses was quite high—she and John both wanted to economize. John planned to stay in Philadelphia as little as possible and retreat to Quincy when Congress was not in session, usually from May through October.

During John's second term as vice president, Abigail stayed behind while John split his time between Philadelphia and his home in Quincy.

Once again, Abigail and John engaged in regular correspondence while they were apart. They discussed politics and foreign policy—debating what role the United States should play in European affairs and whether or not to support the French Revolution. They also shared news of the children. President Washington appointed John Quincy minister to the Netherlands in 1794. Abigail would miss her son, but was delighted with his new position. His brother Thomas would accompany him as secretary.

Meanwhile, Nabby and her family had returned to New York after their time in Europe. Her brother Charles, who was in New York practicing law, soon fell in love with Sally Smith, Nabby's husband's younger sister. Abigail thought he was too young to be a husband, but the couple married anyway.

In 1796, George Washington announced his retirement. This presented an interesting opportunity for John. The vice presidency was not a role he had enjoyed. He thought so much of what he had done was insignificant, but the presidency was an office to which he had often aspired. However, President Washington was such a heroic figure that no one could follow in his footsteps without suffering severe criticism. Although well aware of the difficulties, John and Abigail considered the prospects.

New Federal City

In 1791, President George Washington made plans to establish a permanent U.S. capital on land that had belonged to Maryland and Virginia. He chose Andrew Ellicott, a surveyor, to lay out the streets and appointed architect Pierre Charles L'Enfant to design the new federal city. After sparring with the President, L'Enfant was dismissed and replaced by Ellicott, who revised L'Enfant's original plan.

chapter **10**

On the Road as First Lady

Since John was vice president, he appeared to many to be the logical successor to George Washington. Abigail and John discussed the possibility of his entering the race and weighed his qualifications. His experience as a delegate to the Continental Congresses was proof of his leadership ability, and the time he had spent in Europe

John Adams made no public campaign appearances for the 1796 election, but supporters promoted his candidacy with some unusual objects, such as this pitcher.

had opened his eyes to new ways of thinking. They both believed John was qualified to take on the responsibility. In addition, tensions were growing between the United States and France, and John seemed the most capable of ensuring peace. Life in Quincy was appealing, but they had never shied away from public service in the past. After much deliberation, they agreed that John should run if chosen, and serve if elected.

The two political parties picked their candidates. In recent years, Thomas Jefferson and John Adams had grown apart. They had disagreed over

DEMOCRATIC-REPUBLICAN

The Democratic-Republicans favored states' rights and maintaining favorable relations with France.

political issues. Now they found themselves rivals in the presidential election: Jefferson was nominated by the Democratic-Republicans and Adams by the Federalists.

As in previous elections, the candidates themselves did not campaign, but left this to other politicians whose opinions and speeches were recorded and disseminated by the press. John remained in Quincy and Thomas Jefferson at Monticello, his hilltop home in Virginia.

John was in Philadelphia on December 7, 1796, when the electors (or representatives of the states) met in their home states to cast their votes. As snow, hail, and rain fell in Quincy, Abigail wrote to John, "On the decisions of this day hangs perhaps the destiny of America." Two days later, she proudly reported that all the electors in Massachusetts had voted unanimously for John.

Although the official results were not announced for two months, rumors abounded in the weeks following the

FEDERALIST

The Federalists supported a strong central government and the creation of a national bank.

election. Word started to leak out first that the winner was Thomas Jefferson, and then that it was John Adams. The vote became official in February: John received 71 votes and his opponent 68.

The First Lady's Day

As first lady, Abigail awoke at 5:00 AM to attend to personal and household affairs. At 11:00 AM, she dressed in preparation to receive guests. The family usually dined together at 3:00 PM. Then Abigail went by carriage to call on the wives of government officials. In the evenings, she often hosted dinner for cabinet members, senators, congressmen, and their families. She also followed the Washingtons' tradition of organizing festive New Year's Day and Fourth of July celebrations. Despite the many social obligations of her new position, Abigail also continued to serve as John's principal adviser.

On February 8, 1797, the day the election results were announced in Philadelphia, Abigail was still in Quincy. But the weight of John's future responsibilities was not lost on her. Abigail wrote to John of the importance of justice, impartiality, and "an understanding heart," and of her wish that "the things which make for peace may not be hidden from your eyes."

In preparation for her departure, Abigail located a tenant to take over the farm while she was gone. She also cared for John's mother, who was now seriously ill. Susanna died on April 21, 1797, at the age of 89. A week later, Abigail and her niece Louisa departed for Philadelphia. Stopping on the way to visit with Nabby, Abigail was distressed to learn that the Smiths were having financial troubles. William, who liked to live above his means, had left Nabby alone with the children so that he could pursue yet another business scheme. Abigail was relieved to find her grandchildren were in good health, but she worried that their

father's extravagant lifestyle was a bad influence and she hated to see her daughter so unhappy.

Abigail and Louisa left New York only to find the roads extremely muddy and difficult to traverse. After an exhausting journey, they arrived in the capital on May 10. Abigail spent a few days recovering and then took on a rigorous schedule as first lady. As before, when she'd been the vice president's wife in Philadelphia, much of her day was taken up with official entertaining.

Meanwhile, relations with France had taken a serious turn for the worse. In fact, armed French vessels had attacked American merchant ships. John sent three special envoys, or representatives, to France to negotiate

The conflict between France and the United States would escalate over the coming years. This image depicts a famous 1799 sea battle.

a diplomatic solution, and, at the same time, called for a strengthening of the navy. Upon their arrival in Paris the envoys, at first ignored by the French government, were eventually granted an audience with three secret agents that the Americans called X, Y, and Z. These men demanded a large bribe as well as a promise for a loan before they would agree to negotiate. The American envoys refused. Democratic-Republicans

In 1797 John Quincy Adams was appointed ambassador to Prussia by his father. He married Louisa before starting his duties.

took this as a sign that war was imminent and blamed the president for mishandling the affair. Once again Thomas Jefferson turned against his old friend.

Louisa Catherine Johnson married John Quincy in London, where her father was serving as U.S. consulate general.

Abigail followed the controversy closely and served as John's principal adviser. She also managed the farm from a distance and corresponded regularly with her children, friends, and relatives. She learned belatedly of John Quincy's marriage to Louisa Catherine Johnson, the daughter of an

SEDITION

Sedition is agitation or rebellion against the government.

American merchant, on July 26, 1797, at the All Hallows Barking Church near the Tower of London. (Years earlier, in 1789, Abigail had tried to put an end to John Quincy's first romance—perhaps it came as little surprise that now John Quincy would marry without seeking his parents' permission, or even informing them.)

Although John Adams did not declare war on France, Congress prepared for the possibility and, in 1798, passed what became known as the Alien and Sedition Acts. The Alien Act gave the President the right to expel foreigners considered dangerous. The Sedition Act made "false, scandalous, and malicious" writing against the president or Congress a crime. John Adams did nothing to oppose these measures, even though they seemed to violate the right to freedom of speech guaranteed in the First Amendment to the Constitution—a decision that would lead to severe criticism from the Democratic-Republicans, as well as some members of his own Federalist party. Abigail also supported these acts and wrote to her sister on May 26, 1798, "I wish the laws of our country were competent to punish the stirrer-up of sedition, the writer and printer of base and unfounded calumny. This would contribute as much to the peace and harmony of our country as any measure, and in times like the present, a more careful and attentive

CALUMNY

Calumny is the act of making false charges against a person.

watch ought to be kept over foreigners. This will be done in future if the Alien Bill passes."

When the Adamses returned to Quincy that summer, Abigail had planned to present John with a surprise. She had made arrangements to have a "book room" built—an addition to the house that John could use as a study. Abigail was disappointed to learn that the project had been delayed and was not ready upon their arrival. The summer proved stressful for both of them. The undeclared war with France, which became known as the "Quasi-War," made them anxious. They worried too about their son Charles, who was drinking too much, mishandling his financial affairs, and making his wife and children unhappy. Abigail became ill. She remained in bed for 11 weeks with recurring fevers and suffered from what was most probably another case of malaria. John was distraught. By November, Abigail had started to recover, and John returned to Philadelphia, leaving Abigail in Quincy.

Thomas Adams returned to Philadelphia in January 1799, after spending four years abroad. John Quincy had given him a message to deliver: the French were ready to negotiate. John, greatly relieved, appointed William Vans Murray as ambassador and called on him to end the dispute. Up until this time, the Federalists were planning for war; they had not expected their president to successfully pursue a diplomatic solution. Now it seemed peace was in the offing, though deliberations would continue for many months.

On December 14, 1799, George Washington died from a strep infection and was buried at his home at Mount Vernon, Virginia. The entire country was in mourning. A grand procession and a four-and-a-half hour service were held on December 26 at the German Lutheran Church, the largest church in Philadelphia. Hundreds of citizens came to pay their respects; Abigail and John later received them all in their home. Abigail, who had always admired President Washington for his humility, wrote to her sister, "No man ever lived, more deservedly beloved and respected. The praise and I may say adulation which followed his administration for several years, never made him forget that he was a man, subject to the weakness and frailty attached to human nature. . . . Possessed of power, possessed of an extensive influence, he never used it but for the benefit of his country."

By this time, Congress was finally ready to begin

In this portrait by William Winstanley, John Adams is depicted with all the trappings of power—and wearing the same suit he wore to meet King George III.

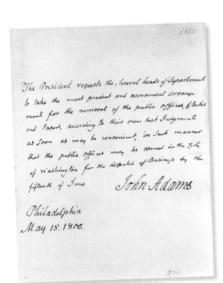

This written order from John Adams directs all government offices to move to Washington.

moving the capital to the new Federal City. Before the Adamses departed for the new site, they gave a party for "28 young or rather unmarried ladies and gentlemen." After dinner, their son Thomas asked if they could dance. Abigail agreed, and the tables were removed to make room. Abigail wrote, "More pleasure, ease and enjoyment I have rarely witnessed. . . . Several of the company declared that they should always remember the evening as one of the pleasantest of their lives." She also commented on the young women's attire: "I wished that more had been left to the imagination, and less to the eye." John retired after an hour, but Abigail "tarried" until midnight.

In May 1800, John traveled to the new Federal City, named "Washington" in honor of the first president. What he found was a small village in a swamp. He spent 10 days at Tunnicliffe's City Hotel near the unfinished Capitol building. He toured the President's House—also under construction— and visited Martha Washington at Mount Vernon. He then headed north again, this time to Quincy, where he would join Abigail for the summer.

John would return to Washington the following October, this time to stay. Although progress had been made, the President's House appeared far from complete. Abigail left Quincy in November. On her way to Washington, she stopped in New York to see Charles, who had become quite ill, due mainly to alcohol abuse. It was hard for Abigail to see her son in pain, but she was grateful to Nabby for taking care of him.

Abigail found the President's House "in a beautiful situation in front of which is the Potomac with a view of Alexandria. The country around is romantic but . . . a wilderness at present." The surrounding area was "a quagmire after every rain" so it would be hard to travel, and she called the nearby city of Georgetown "the dirtiest hole I ever saw." She told her sister that the President's House was "built for ages to come"—but that, since not

The architect of the President's House in Washington was selected in a competition. George Washington chose Irish-born James Hoban, a resident of Charleston, South Carolina.

A Work in Progress

George Washington enlarged Hoban's original floorplan by about 30%—thus beginning a tradition of presidents adapting the home to suit their needs and their times. The first toilet was installed in 1833 for Andrew Jackson. Rutherford B. Hayes had the first telephone put in. And the name White House became official under Theodore Roosevelt.

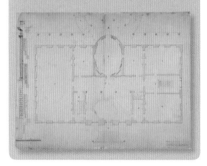

one room was finished, she would rather live in Philadelphia. The rooms were so damp that they had to keep 13 fires going. Still, she was "determined to be satisfied and content, to say nothing of inconvenience."

The 1800 election again pitted John Adams against Thomas Jefferson. James Callender, an influential newspaper writer, was determined to help elect Jefferson. Although the president had worked hard to make peace his primary goal, Callender published stories ridiculing John, calling him a warmonger on the one hand, and weak and repulsive on the other.

In early November, John learned that his diplomatic mission to France had succeeded. French ruler Napoleon Bonaparte had agreed to the Treaty of Mortefontaine; peace became official when the U.S. Senate approved the treaty in December. The Quasi-War had finally come to an end. The peace that John had attained would give him great pleasure for the remainder of his years.

Unfortunately, this achievement would not assure John victory in the next election, nor would it influence the results. By the time peace with France was declared, the electors' minds were already made up. John received 65 votes, but his rivals Thomas Jefferson and Aaron Burr each received 73 votes. The House of Representatives would determine the outcome of the tie, and Thomas Jefferson would become the third president.

Meanwhile, Abigail and John learned that their son Charles had died. In the weeks after Abigail's visit, his condition had deteriorated and "his mind at times was much deranged." Abigail and John deeply regretted the last years of Charles's life. "He was beloved, in spite of his errors," Abigail wrote. Charles left behind his wife, Sally, and two young daughters, Susanna and Abigail. In the months and years to come, Abigail would take in Sally and the children to comfort and care for them.

When Abigail moved into the President's House, it was still under construction. She hung the laundry out to dry in the East Room.

chapter **11**
Back to Quincy

Before leaving Washington, Abigail and John had several good-byes to say. They held the traditional New Year's Day reception at the President's House and, a few days later, asked Thomas Jefferson to join them for dinner. Abigail's health was poor and she was again suffering from rheumatism and a fever, but she still held an elaborate dinner party for her friends. Three weeks later, a group of judges and cabinet appointees dined with her.

On February 13, 1801, Abigail began the 500-mile (805-km) journey home. The near-freezing temperatures made the roads treacherous, and several rivers had to be forded. John did not leave until March 4,

Shown here around the time of the Adamses' departure, the President's House was cold, damp, and surrounded by mud. The Adamses made it more inviting by lighting fires in every fireplace.

the day of Thomas Jefferson's inauguration. Eager to return home, he didn't wait for the new president to give his speech—a decision that would later draw criticism.

Abigail had told her sister that John was prepared to withdraw from public life and hoped "to be a good farmer yet." But the change in routine would not come easily. John had never spent long stretches of time in Quincy without focusing

Gilbert Stuart painted portraits of John and Abigail before they left the White House. John had them hung at their home in Quincy.

on politics or government. The defeat in the national election had also hurt his pride. And, like Abigail, he was suffering from the loss of their son Charles.

The issues John faced would never again be of such wide scope, but his life—and Abigail's—would be very full. In 1800, they had added a new wing to Peacefield, which included a formal parlor for entertaining called the Long Room and more bedrooms on the third floor. John's book room on the second floor had also finally been completed. The farm needed tending, however,

Gilbert Stuart started this portrait in 1800. Abigail thought the artist made her look much younger than she was.

and John played an active role. A diary entry from August 1804 reads, "The last week in August we ploughed a ditch and brought the earth into the yard and 32 loads of mud from the cove."

As usual, there were many people to care for: John and Abigailt's niece Louisa Smith was living with them, and their widowed daughter-in-law Sally Smith Adams had brought her two children to stay at Peacefield. With William away much of the time, Nabby and her children often visited, too. But the household did not seem complete without a dog, so the family soon adopted a Newfoundland puppy. At last, it seemed the Adamses had found the retreat they had dreamed of. John wrote that their home was christened Peacefield in honor of "the peace which I assisted in making in 1783,

Peacefield was a happy retreat for John and Abigail, who were surrounded by family there.

of the thirteen years peace and neutrality which I have contributed to preserve, and of the constant peace and tranquility which I have enjoyed in this residence."

This watch belonged to Abigail and was treasured by her children and grandchildren.

In September 1801, after seven years in Europe, John Quincy, his wife Louisa, and their newborn son, George Washington Adams, returned to the United States. John Quincy came immediately to Peacefield to see his parents. He brought with him a present for Abigail—tiles purchased in Liverpool, which Abigail had installed around the fireplace in the bedroom. Louisa and George went first to Washington to visit Louisa's parents and later joined John Quincy at Peacefield.

Even when John Quincy and his family moved into their own house in Boston, they spent long weekends with John and Abigail. After John Quincy was elected to the U.S. Senate in 1803, he and Louisa tried different living arrangements. At first, George stayed with his grandparents and Louisa accompanied John Quincy to Washington. Later, Louisa also stayed in Quincy, and her husband traveled back and forth.

At this point, Thomas was practicing law in Philadelphia, but Abigail wanted her youngest son closer.

Thomas Boylston Adams and his wife, Nancy, lived at Peacefield and later moved into the house where Thomas's father had been born.

She did her best to persuade him to move and, with coaxing from John Quincy, he finally agreed. In 1805, after Thomas married Nancy Harrod, a young woman from Haverhill, the newlyweds joined Abigail and John at Peacefield.

Abigail had often regretted that her family was so scattered while the children were young. She now took great pleasure in having so much family at home. Every Sunday, she hosted a big dinner, with plentiful food and animated conversation. John enjoyed it as much as she did.

In the summer of 1809, President James Madison named John Quincy ambassador to Russia. John Quincy's two older children, George and John, would split their time between Peacefield and the home of Abigail's sister, Mary. His youngest son, Charles, would accompany his parents to St. Petersburg. Abigail felt "the keenest anguish"

"You were not born for yourself, but to fill every hour with some useful employment."

–Abigail Adams, in a letter to her granddaughter

at the sudden separation. Communication would be difficult—just as it had been when John was in Europe.

Over the years, several of Abigail's grandchildren came and went from Peacefield, some staying for a few months and others for years. Abigail kept in touch with those who were not close by and encouraged them to write long letters.

She thanked Caroline, the youngest of Nabby's children, for writing during a trip: "A letter from a traveling friend is a great treat to those who sit by their firesides." She then added, "I think of you more on Sunday than on any other day," and advised Caroline to spend that day "in a useful manner" if it was not possible to attend public worship.

Abigail's letters reflected her continued interest in public affairs. As always, she also wrote about whatever was on her mind—her family, the farm, the garden.

John Quincy Adams

John Quincy Adams began his political career at age 26, as minister to the Netherlands. Over the course of the next three decades, he held a series of high-profile diplomatic positions, and even served as a U.S. senator. In 1829, he was elected president of the United States. Unlike his father, he continued his political career after he left office, serving in the U.S. House of Representatives for 17 years.

And she was quick to dispense advice: "You were not born for yourself, but to fill every hour with some useful employment," she wrote in a letter to Caroline.

When Abigail learned Caroline had taken up the spinning wheel, she praised her for her new skill: "The more we are qualified to help ourselves, the less dependent we are upon others." Abigail admired Caroline's self-sufficiency, a quality she shared with her granddaughter and one that had been put to the test many times as John's work pulled him away from her.

In 1811, Nabby became seriously ill and came to Quincy to seek advice from the family doctor, Benjamin Rush. He

diagnosed her with breast cancer and recommended a mastectomy (the surgical removal of a breast)— a procedure still quite rare at the time. Nabby consented and endured the operation without an anesthetic. She and her daughter Caroline spent the winter with Abigail

Dr. Benjamin Rush served in the Second Continental Congress and was active in the movement to abolish slavery. He remained a good friend to the Adams family.

> "Yesterday completed half a century since I entered the married state . . . I have great cause for thankfulness."
>
> –Abigail Adams, in a letter to her granddaughter

and John before returning to New York.

Two years later, Nabby suffered a recurrence and came home to Quincy, along with her husband and children. She passed away a few weeks later, on August 15, 1813. Abigail and John were heartbroken. Eighteen-year-old Caroline remained at Peacefield to help look after her grandparents.

The following year, in the Long Room at Peacefield, Caroline married her brother's good friend John De Windt. Abigail provided the wedding supper: hams, chickens, pies, puddings, and wedding cake. In October 1814, Abigail wrote to her granddaughter, "Yesterday completed half a century since I entered the married state, then just your age. I have great cause for thankfulness." Her "greatest source of unhappiness," she said, came from the "long and cruel separations" that she and her young family had endured "in a time of war." Yet she had always given her full-fledged support to the cause that led to these separations.

Abigail took great pleasure in assuring Caroline that the American government would "promote the happiness and prosperity of the people, where liberty and independence were so well understood, and amply enjoyed" in a country she had helped create.

chapter **12**
Peacefield

For six years, George and John remained in Quincy and enjoyed the company of their aging grandparents. But John Quincy and Louisa, who had both lived abroad during their youth, missed their sons and wanted them to share the experience of living in a foreign country. In 1815, they arranged for the boys to join them in Europe.

Two years later, to Abigail and John's great delight, the newly elected president James Monroe appointed John Quincy secretary of state. By this time, the young Adams family was happy to return home. Upon arrival at Peacefield, John jumped out of the carriage first, and George was right behind, shouting, "O Grandmother." The youngest child, Charles, not having seen his grandparents in eight years, appeared frightened, but his shyness quickly wore off. When John Quincy and Louisa left for Washington, the three boys stayed behind. George attended Harvard while his brothers went to school in Boston; all of them made frequent weekend visits to Quincy.

Once again Abigail, was hosting large dinners. Her good humor and "sunny spirit" were much admired. But in October 1818, she fell ill with typhoid fever. The social gatherings came to a halt. The doctor administered quinine, used at the time to reduce fever. Abigail started to improve, and

then, unexpectedly, grew worse. As she lay in bed at Peacefield, John, her niece Louisa, and others sat by her side. In terrible

> *"She did not wish to live any longer than she could be useful."*
>
> –Harriet Welsh, about Abigail Adams

pain, knowing she was dying, Abigail said she "did not wish to live any longer than she could be useful." John could not bear to see her suffering and asked, "Shall I pray for a stroke of lightning that killed my friend Otis?" He wanted to lie down beside her and die, too. Although she continued to take quinine, it didn't work as the doctor had hoped, and on October 28, Abigail died at home. She was 73 years old.

Harriet Welsh, a cousin, wrote that after Abigail's death there was "scarcely an inhabitant of Quincy who [did] not wear a black ribbon." The governor, lieutenant-governor, and Reverend John Kirkland, president of Harvard College, were among the pallbearers. Reverend Kirkland spoke at the burial service. He remembered Abigail for her "cheerful, grateful heart" and he recalled her strength in facing adversity. Although she moved in the "highest walks of society," she was "never led for a moment to forget the feelings and the claims of others."

One obituary notice called Abigail an "enlightened woman" and a most "affectionate and faithful mother," and praised her "understanding and heart," her sound judgment and brilliant imagination, her intelligent conversation, and her famous "flashes of wit." Another notice spoke of her relationship with John: "She was admitted at all times to share largely of his thoughts. . . . She was a friend, whom it was his delight to consult in every perplexity of public affairs."

John Quincy, then in Washington, wished he could be by his father's side. "What must it be to my father, and how will he support life without her who has been to him its charm?" he wrote in his diary on the day of his mother's burial. Indeed, John was grief-stricken. Assuming he would not have long to live, he wrote to his son that his separation from Abigail would not "be so long . . . as twenty separations heretofore. . . . The pangs and the anguish have not been so great as when you and and I embarked for France in 1778."

Thomas Jefferson, who had long ago lost his wife and five of his six children, wrote to John, "The same trials have taught me that for ills so immeasurable, time and silence are the only medicines." After a long period of alienation, John and Jefferson had started writing each other again several years earlier.

As secretary of state to President James Monroe, John Quincy was in Washington when his mother died.

The renewed friendship was now a great comfort for John. Their lengthy correspondence would continue to be a source of great pleasure for both men in their old age.

"[There is] scarcely an inhabitant of Quincy who does not wear a black ribbon."

–Harriet Welsh, upon the death of Abigail Adams

In 1824, John Quincy Adams ran as the Democratic-Republican candidate for president. When none of the four candidates received a majority, the election was thrown to the House of Representatives. John Quincy eventually emerged the winner to become the sixth president of the United States. He had followed in his father's footsteps, and John, though he could not have been more pleased, wished that Abigail could have shared his joy.

Thomas Jefferson also took pleasure in knowing that the son of his old friend had been elected president. He recalled the wonderful times he had spent with the Adamses in Paris. He knew how proud John must feel of his son. "I sincerely congratulate you on the high gratification which the issue of the late election must have afforded you," he wrote.

John replied, "Every line from you exhilarates my spirits and gives me a glow of pleasure, but your kind congratulations are a solid comfort to my heart." He ended his letters with these words: "I look back with rapture to those golden days when Virginia and Massachusetts lived and acted together like a band of brothers."

Gilbert Stuart painted this portrait of John Adams in 1823. John died three years later, on the Fourth of July.

In his old age, John could not hear or see very well. Still, he spent long hours in his book room and occasionally entertained a visitor with a story from the past. Looking back on his life, John, at the age of 90, wrote to his granddaughter Caroline, "At this time it seems to me to have been wicked to have left such a wife and such a family as I did, but it was done in the service of my country." The long separations had been difficult, but both Abigail and John always believed that the sacrifices they made served a purpose, and that the country—and future generations—were well served by them. If Abigail had asked John to stay with her in Quincy, he would have agreed. It was she who chose to let him go.

In July 1826, both John and Thomas Jefferson became ill. Jefferson, at the age of 83, fell in and out of consciousness, but he was determined to live until the Fourth of July, the 50th anniversary of the Declaration of Independence. He received his wish, passing away at 1:00 PM on July 4. John, at home in Massachusetts, died that evening at the end of a summer storm. He was 90 years old. "Thomas Jefferson still lives" are reputed to be his last words. He would never know he was mistaken.

The day had started with the roar of cannons to celebrate the country's independence; it ended that evening with the roll of thunder. Three days later, on July 7, 4,000 people would come out to attend John's burial service.

First Parish Church

John's role in the Continental Congress will not be forgotten, nor will his efforts to create an independent nation. Without his voice in Congress—his revolutionary zeal—the delegates might not have had the courage to move forward. John went on to display great diplomatic skill in Europe and leadership at home.

Abigail was the support and "dearest friend" who helped John reach the

John and Abigail were buried in the graveyard of the Quincy First Parish Church. When John died, the church was in the process of being rebuilt, using granite he had donated. In 1828, John Quincy Adams moved his parents's coffins to the crypt of the new church. John Quincy and Louisa Catherine Adams now rest beside John and Abigail.

The Stone Library

Peacefield's Stone Library houses the Adams family's collection of 12,000 books and manuscripts. Charles Francis Adams compiled and edited his grandfather's writing, letters from his grandparents, and John Quincy Adams's memoirs at the oak table now on view at the library. The library and many Adams artifacts can be viewed by visitors to Peacefield, which is now a preserved historic site.

greatest heights. She will be remembered for this and also for her own strengths. Self-reliant, she raised her family and managed the farm for the many years that John was away during and after the war. Brave and caring, she inspired her family and friends to stand up for their beliefs, and found time to comfort them in time of need. Spirited and witty, she brought cheer to all around her.

Abigail started writing at a young age, and she never stopped. She used her pen to reflect on—and influence—the course of history. Writing for family and friends, she included descriptions of everyday life, revealed deep feelings, and developed well-constructed arguments. Her letters to John—and his to her—tell a beautiful love story, filled with longing, tension, devotion, humor, and joy. Abigail could be flirtatious, and she could also be passionate.

An advocate for women, Abigail encouraged John to stand up for women's rights. She spoke out not only for political freedom, but for the education of girls. Her own life was a testament to hard work and perseverance. She was frugal when the war required it. She was also a gracious host in Europe, as first lady, and at Peacefield. And she was always generous, opening her home to the refugees from Boston during the war, and later to her extended family and large circle of friends.

In her letters, Abigail expressed herself with great clarity as well as compassion. Only on occasion did she reveal a dark mood; she almost always had a positive outlook. Little did she know that her letters would become such an inspiration—and a great gift—to the world, offering future generations a portrait of a minister's daughter, the wife of one president and the mother of another, a record of the birth of a nation, and a window into the character of an independent and loving woman.

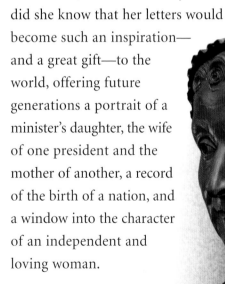

This sculpture by artist Meredith Bergmann pays tribute to the life of Abigail Adams. It is part of the Boston Women's Memorial.

Events in the Life of Abigail Adams

August–October 1774
Abigail manages the farm in Braintree while John serves in the First Continental Congress in Philadelphia.

November 22, 1744
Abigail is born to Elizabeth and William Smith at the parsonage in Weymouth, Massachusetts.

July 18, 1776
Abigail hears the Declaration of Independence read aloud from the balcony of the Boston State House.

October 25, 1764
Abigail marries John Adams, a young lawyer from Braintree, Massachusetts.

1780–1784
Abigail sells goods imported from Europe and China.

July 1767
Abigail, John, and their children Nabby and John Quincy move from Braintree to Boston.

April 19, 1775
The first battles of the American Revolution are fought at Lexington and Concord.

July 12, 1776
Abigail takes her children, Nabby, John Quincy, Charles, and Thomas to Boston for smallpox inoculations.

March 5, 1770
Five colonists are killed by British soldiers in the Boston Massacre; John later agrees to represent the British soldiers.

June 17, 1775
From Braintree, Abigail and her son John Quincy watch the Battle of Bunker Hill.

November 1779
John, accompanied by his sons John Quincy and Charles, travels to Paris to negotiate a peace treaty with Great Britain.

September 3, 1783
The Treaty of Paris, signed by John Adams, officially ends the American Revolution.

November 1800
Abigail and John move into the President's House in Washington, the new capital.

October 25, 1814
Abigail and John celebrate their 50th wedding anniversary at Peacefield.

May 1785
John, Abigail, and Nabby settle in London.

June 12, 1786
Nabby marries William Stephens Smith at her parents' home in London.

Autumn 1790
Abigail and John move to Philadelphia, the new capital city.

February 1825
John Quincy Adams is elected as the sixth U.S. president.

June 20, 1784
Abigail and Nabby set sail for Europe where they will be reunited with John.

March 1789
George Washington is elected as the first U.S. president, and John Adams as the first vice president.

March 1797
John Adams becomes the second U.S. president.

October 28, 1818
Abigail dies of typhoid fever.

July 4, 1826
Both John Adams and Thomas Jefferson die on the 50th anniversary of the Declaration of Independence.

June 1788
John and Abigail return to the United States and move into a new home in Braintree, to be called Peacefield.

124

Index

Bibliography

Adams, Charles Francis, ed. *Familiar Letters of John Adams and His Wife Abigail Adams, During the Revolution, with a Memoir of Mrs. Adams.* Freeport, New York: Books for Libraries Press, 1875. Reprinted 1970.

Adams Family Papers: An Electronic Archive. Massachusetts Historical Society. http://www.masshist.org/digitaladams/

Adams Family Papers [microform reels #438, 445], Massachusetts Historical Society.

Adams, John Quincy. *Memoirs of John Quincy Adams,* edited by Charles Francis Adams. Philadelphia: J. P. Lippincott, 1875.

The Adams Papers: Adams Family Correspondence Vols. I-VIII, edited by L. H. Butterfield, with Wendell D. Garrett and Marjorie E. Sprague. Cambridge: Belknap Press of Harvard University Press, 1963.

The Adams Papers: Diary and Autobiography of John Adams (includes *Abigail Adams' diary*), Vol. 1, 2, 3, 4, edited by L. H. Butterfield, with Leonard C. Faber and Wendell D. Garrett. Cambridge: The Belknap Press of Harvard University Press, 1961–1962.

The Adams Papers: The Earliest Diary of John Adams, edited by L. H. Butterfield, with Wendell D. Garrett and Marc Friedlaender. Cambridge: the Belknap Press of Harvard University Press, 1966.

Adams-Welsh collection, Massachusetts Historical Society.

Bober, Natalie S., *Abigail Adams: Witness to a Revolution.* New York: Atheneum Books for Young Readers, 1995.

Cappon, Lester J., ed. *The Adams-Jefferson Letters.* Chapel Hill: University of North Carolina Press, 1959, 1988.

Diggins, John Patrick, ed. *The Portable John Adams.* New York: Penguin Group, 2004.

Kalman, Bobbie. *The Kitchen (Historic Communities series).* Crabtree Publishing Company, 1990.

Levin, Phyllis Lee. *Abigail Adams: A Biography.* New York: St. Martin's Press, 1987.

McCullough, David. *John Adams.* New York: Simon & Schuster, 2001.

Miller, Lillian B. *In the Minds and Hearts of the People: Prologue to the American Revolution, 1760-1774.* New York Graphic Society, 1974.

———. *"The Dye Is Now Cast" The Road to American Independence, 1774-1776.* Published for the National Portrait Gallery by the Smithsonian Institution Press, 1975.

Mitchell, Stewart, ed. *New Letters of Abigail Adams, 1788–1801.* Boston: Houghton Mifflin Company, 1947.

Roberts, Cokie. *Founding Mothers: The Women Who Raised Our Nation.* New York: HarperCollins, 2004.

Shackelford, George Green. *Thomas Jefferson's Travels in Europe, 1784-1789.* Baltimore: The Johns Hopkins University Press, 1995.

Shuffelton, Frank, ed. *The Letters of John and Abigail Adams.* New York: Penguin Books, 2004.

Smith, Abigail Adams. *Journal and correspondence of Miss Adams, daughter of John Adams, second president of the United States. Written in France and England, in 1785. Ed. by her daughter, Caroline Amelia Smith De Windt. (Vol. 2: Correspondence of Miss Adams).* New York: Wiley & Putnam, 1841-2.

Warren, Mercy Otis. *History of the Rise, Progress and Termination of the American Revolution.* Edited and annotated by Lester H. Cohen. Boston: Manning and Loring, 1805.

Wilstach, Paul, ed. *Correspondence of John Adams and Thomas Jefferson, 1812-1826.* Indianapolis: The Bobs-Merrill Company, 1925.

Withey, Lynne. *Dearest Friend: A Life of Abigail Adams.* New York: Free Press, 1981.

For Further Study

The Adams National Historical Park in Quincy, Massachusetts, is comprised of John Adams' birthplace, the house next door where Abigail and John lived and their children were born, and Peacefield where the family moved after the Adamses returned from Europe in 1788. See http://www.nps.gov/adam/ for more information and photographs.

Also in Quincy is the United First Parish Church, called the Hancock Meeting House. You may visit the church and the crypt, the final resting place for Abigail and John, as well as John Quincy and Louisa Adams.

Five miles (8 km) away is Abigail Adams's birthplace in Weymouth, Massachusetts, where Abigail spent her childhood. She and John were also married here. See http://www.abigailadamsbirthplace.org/

Abigail and John's letters, diaries, and papers are housed at the Massachusetts Historical Society in Boston. For more information about the Adams family and their correspondence, see http://www.masshist.org/adams/

The HBO miniseries *John Adams* (2008), starring Paul Giamatti and Laura Linney, tells the story of both John and Abigail. It is an excellent adaptation of David McCullough's biography—fast-paced and compelling.

Author's Note

One might say this book began in the summer of 1972 when I worked as a research assistant in Boston for Lillian B. Miller, Historian of the National Portrait Gallery. She was writing *In the Minds and Hearts of the People: Prologue to the American Revolution, 1770-1774* and I was charged with notating artifacts from the period. Special thanks go to her and to Evelyn Kem Knapp and Betsy Ivey Sawyer for sharing their love of history. To Beth Hester for excellent advice and thoughtful editing and for giving me the opportunity to do this work. To Sara Martin at the Massachusetts Historical Society for careful reading and perceptive comments. To the staff at the Massachusetts Historical Society for graciously sharing their knowledge and facility. To Karen Yourell, who guided me through Abigail's homes and took me up to Penn's Hill. To my students, friends, and colleagues at the Corcoran College of Art + Design. To Kate, Brian, Eve, Dan, and Ida—my dearest readers—and those soon to be dearest readers, Karenna and Jack. And to Jon, my traveling companion and dearest friend.

Works Cited

Unless otherwise indicated, quotations from the letters of Abigail and John Adams are taken from *Familiar Letters of John Adams and His Wife Abigail Adams,* edited by Charles Francis Adams.

p. 6: "Charlestown…cannot eat, drink, or sleep" 18 June 1775, pp. 67–8

p. 7: "The day…depends" 18 June 1775, p. 67

p. 7: "The spirits…drop in the bucket." 18 June 1775, p. 68

p. 10: "never to speak…conversation" *Adams Family Correspondence, vol. II,* p. 306

p. 11: "lively, cheerful disposition," "instruction and amusement" p. xii

p. 12: "a meditative, imaginative mind" p. ix

p. 16: "growing curiosity… " *Diary and Autobiography of John Adams, vol. 3,* p. 261

p. 19: "no freeman should…" *Boston Gazette,* 14 Oct. 1765, reprinted in *Portable John Adams,* p. 229

p. 26: "It is a fundamental…influence at all left" 6 July 1774, p. 16

p. 26: "Great things… " 6 July 1774, p. 18

p. 27: "Your task…prosper you."15 Aug 1774, p. 23

p. 27: "The great distance…since you left me." 19 Aug 1774, p. 25

p. 27: "The tenderest regard…" 2 Sept 1774, p. 30

p. 28: "entertain a fondness for it." 19 Aug 1774, p. 26

p. 28: "the education of our children…not little and frivolous." 28 Aug 1774, p. 28

p. 28: "My babes…from my heart."14 Sept 1774, p 33

p. 29: "There is in the Congress…" 8 Sept 1774, p. 29

p. 29: "If there is distress…" 8 Sept 1774, p. 31

p. 30: "Tell all my clerks…" 7 Oct 1774, p. 44

p. 30: "I long impatiently…" 19 Aug 1774, p. 26

p. 30: "The maxim…throughout the country." 24 Sept 1774, p. 41

p. 30: "But let them avoid war *if possible—if possible,* I say." 7 Oct 1774, p. 44

p. 31: "My time is totally filled…" 14 Sept 1774, p. 32

p. 31: "I had rather give a dollar…" 14 Sept 1774, p. 33

p. 31: "tedious beyond expression" 9 Oct 1774, p. 45

p. 33: "in case of real danger…with our children." 2 May 1775, p. 52

p. 33: "I felt very anxious…a heart of lead." 4 May 1775, p. 53

p. 36: "the modesty…his face." 16 July 1775, p. 79

p. 36: "You would laugh…" *Adams Family Papers.* 25 June 1775 [electronic edition]

p. 37: "The writing is very scant…" 5 July 1775, p. 73

p. 37: "It gives me more pleasure…" 7 July 1775, p. 77

p. 37: "It was the longest and best letter" 25 July 1775, pp. 85–6

p. 38: "O my bursting heart…" 1 Oct 1775, p. 102

p. 38: "Remember a great deal…" 25 Oct 1775, Abigail Adams Smith, *vol. 2,* p. 3

p. 38: "Child, I see your mother…" 21 Oct 1775, p. 114

p. 39: "All these must go" 7 Oct 1775, p. 105

p. 39: "If we separate from Britain…swallow up the small?" 27 Nov 1775, pp. 125-6

p. 39: "My pen…I never could have talked" 22 Oct 1775, p. 115

p. 40: "I have been happy…unthankful offices: Abigail Adams to Mercy Otis Warren, Jan. 1776, *Adams Family Correspondence, vol. I,* p 423

p. 40: "no prospect…" 18 Feb 1776, p. 135

p. 41: "My God…" 16 Mar 1776, p. 142

p. 42: "remember the ladies…" 31 Mar 1776, pp. 149–50

p. 43: "In practice…" 14 Apr 1776, p. 155

p. 43: "I cannot say…" 7 May 1776, p. 169

pp. 43–44: "I think…use his wife ill." Abigail Adams to Mercy Otis Warren, 27 April 1776, *Adams Family Correspondence, vol. I,* pp. 396–397

p. 44: "happiness…government" from *Thoughts on Government,* reprinted in *Portable,* p. 234

p. 44: "empire of laws, and not of men" from *Thoughts on Government,* reprinted in *Portable,* p. 235

p. 44: "laws…extravagant" from *Thoughts on Government,* reprinted in *Portable,* p. 240

p. 44: "You shine as a stateswoman…" 27 May 1776, p. 177

p. 47: "whichever was debated in America…" 3 July 1776, p. 191

pp. 48–49: "Posterity…" 26 Apr 1777, p. 265

p. 48: "Your sentiments…" 25 Aug 1776, pp. 218–9

p. 49: "I feel as if…" 8 Feb 1777, p. 243

p. 50: "not more than half that time…" 5 Aug 1777, p. 288

p. 51: "How my heart…" 21 Sept 1777, p. 311

p. 51: "Our frying-pans…sword" 13 Apr 1777, p. 259

p. 54: "Great learning…" 10 June 1778, p. 335

p. 55: "Nature and art…" 3 June1778, p. 333

p. 55: "By the mountains of snow…" and "How lonely…" 27 Dec 1778, pp. 350–1

p. 58: "I must study politics and war…music, architecture…." no date, 1780, p. 381

p. 59: "Charles is as well beloved…" no date, 1780, p. 380

p. 60: "peace and domestic happiness…" 9 Dec 1781, p. 401

p. 62: "I have lived to see…" 13 Nov 1782, p. 408

p. 62: "I have too much tenderness…" 13 Aug 1783, Abigail Adams Smith, *vol. 1,* p. 203.

p. 63: "Whether there should be peace or war…" 28 Dec 1782, p. 412

p. 63: "I am determined… receive your old friend." 18 Feb 1783, p. 413

p. 64: "tears rolled down her aged cheek" 20 June 1784, *Diary and Autobiography of John Adams, vol. 3,* p. 154

p. 64: "You who have never tried…" 23 June 1784, *Diary and Autobiography of John Adams, vol. 3,* p. 157.

p. 65: "I am more and more of the mind that a lady ought not to go to sea" 1 July 1784, *Diary and Autobiography of John Adams, vol. 3,* p. 160

p. 66: "When I entered…" Abigail Adams Smith, *vol. 1,* p. viii

p. 67: "I need not…" 17 July 1784, Abigail Adams Smith, *vol. 1,* p. 3

p. 74: "Sir, your words…" 1 June 1785, Abigail Adams Smith, *vol. 1,* p. 78

p. 79: "If politeness and attention…" 23 Aug 1786, Abigail Adams Smith, *vol. 2,* p. 57

p. 80: "rough as a sailor…against her will" 6 July 1787, *Adams-Jefferson Letters,* pp. 183–4

p. 81: "O! now I have learnt to love you…" 20 May 1804, *Adams-Jefferson Letters,* p. 269

p. 82: "I don't like…" 2 April 1788, *Adams Family Correspondence, vol. VIII,* p. 251

pp. 82–83: "I have no other daughter" 27 April 1788, *Adams Family Correspondence, vol. VIII,* p. 247

p. 83: "I hope and pray…" 29 May 1788, Abigail Adams Smith, *vol. 2,* p. 7

p. 83: "Indeed I have seen…" *Diary and Autobiography of John Adams, vol. 3,* p. 215

p. 85: "a spice of fun…gentleman of them all." Abigail Adams Smith, *vol. 2,* p. 87.

pp. 88–89: "I found myself…" 12 July 1789, *New Letters,* p. 15

p. 89: "dotingly fond…" 11 Oct 1789, *New Letters,* p. 30

pp. 89–90: "Can you really believe…" 3 April 1790, *New Letters,* p. 43

p. 90: "I feel low spirited…satisfaction. 3 Oct 1790, *New Letters,* p. 59

p. 90: "My separation from Mrs. Smith…" 10 Oct 1790, *New Letters,* p. 60

p. 91: "This you may be sure…" 5 Feb1792, *New Letters,* p. 77

pp. 91–92: "Indeed my dear Sister…" 29 March 1792, *New Letters,* p. 80

p. 95: "On the decisions of this day…" *Adams Family Papers*

7 Dec 1796 [electronic edition]

p. 96: "an understanding heart…" p. xxvi

pp. 99–100: "I wish the laws…" 26 May 1798, *New Letters*, p. 179

p. 101: "No man ever lived…" 22 Dec 1799, *New Letters*, p. 222

p. 102: "28 young men …less to the eye." 26 April 1800, *New Letters*, pp. 247–8

p. 103: "in a beautiful situation…inconvenience" 21 Nov 1800, *New Letters*, pp. 257–8

p. 105: "his mind…in spite of his errors," 8 Dec 1800, *New Letters*, pp. 261–2

p. 107: "to be a good farmer yet." 15 Jan 1801, *New Letters*, p. 264

p. 108: "The last week in August…" John Adams diary 46, *Adams Family Papers* Aug 1804 [electronic edition]

p. 110: "the keenest anguish" Abigail Adams to Caroline De Windt, 12 Aug 1809, Abigail Adams Smith, *vol. 1*, p. 217

p. 111: "A letter from a traveling friend…" 24 Jan 1808, Abigail Adams Smith, *vol. 1*, pp. 209–210

p. 112: "You were not born…" 2 Feb 1809, Abigail Adams Smith, *vol. 1*, p. 215

p. 112: "The more we are qualified…" 9 Dec 1809, Abigail Adams Smith, *vol. 1*, p. 219

p. 113: "Yesterday completed half a century…" 23 Oct 1814, Abigail Adams Smith, *vol. 1*, p. 229

p. 113: "promote the happiness…" 19 Feb 1815, Abigail Adams Smith, *vol. 1*, p. 232

p. 114: "O Grandmother" 18 Aug 1817, Abigail Adams to Harriet Welsh, Adams Family Papers [microfilm reel #438]

p. 114: "sunny spirit." p. xxviii

p. 115: "she did not wish to live…Shall I pray…" letter from Harriet Welsh to Caroline De Windt, Nov 1818, Adams Family Papers [microform reel #445]

p. 115: "scarcely an inhabitant…ribbon," letter from Harriet Welsh to Caroline De Windt, Nov. 1818, Adams Family Papers [microform reel #445]

p. 115: "cheerful, grateful heart" p. xxix

p. 115: "highest walks of society…claims of others" 12 Nov 1818. obituary notice, Adams Family Papers [microform reel #445]

p. 115: "enlightened woman…flashes of wit" 12 Nov 1818. obituary notice, Adams Family Papers [microform reel #445]

p. 116: "She was admitted…public affairs" obituary notice [1818], Adams/Welsh correspondence, loose papers, Massachusetts Historical Society

p. 116: "What must it be to my father…" *Memoirs of John Quincy Adams, vol. 4* p. 155

p. 116: "be so long…" 11 Nov 1818, Adams Family Papers [microform reel #445]

p. 116: "The same trials…" 13 Nov 1818, *Adams-Jefferson Letters*, p. 529

p. 117: "I sincerely congratulate…" 15 Feb 1825, *Adams-Jefferson Letters*, p. 609

p. 117: "Every line from you…" *Adams-Jefferson Letters*, p. 609

p. 118: "At this time…" Abigail Adams Smith, *vol. 1*, p. vii

—Citations from letters to and from Thomas Jefferson are taken from *The Adams-Jefferson Letters: The Complete Correspondence Between Thomas Jefferson and Abigail and John Adams*, edited by Lester J. Cappon. Copyright (c) 1959 by the University of North Carolina Press, renewed 1987 by Stanley B. Cappon. Used by permission of the publisher.

—Citations from *New Letters of Abigail Adams 1788-1801*, edited with an introduction by Stewart Mitchell, are used by permission of the publisher American Antiquarian Society (Worcester, Mass.), 1949).

—Citations from the Adams-Welsh collection, the Adams Family papers (microfilm), and the *Adams Family Papers: An Electronic Archive* are used by permission of the Massachusetts Historical Society.

—Citations from *The Adams Papers* published by the Belknap Press: Reprinted by permission of the publisher from *The Adams Papers: Diary and Autobiography of John Adams: Volume 3*, edited by L. H. Butterfield, with Leonard C. Faber and Wendell J. Garrett, pp. 154, 157, 160, 215, 261. Cambridge, Mass.: The Belknap Press of Harvard University Press, Copyright 1962 by the Massachusetts Historical Society. Reprinted by permission of the publisher from *The Adams Papers: The Adams Family Correspondence: Volumes 1-2*, edited by L. H. Butterfield, with Wendell D. Garrett and Marjorie E. Sprague, pp. 396-397, 423, 306. Cambridge, Mass.: The Belknap Press of Harvard University Press, Copyright 1963 by the Massachusetts Historical Society. Reprinted by permission of the publisher from *The Adams Papers: The Adams Family Correspondence: Volume 8*, edited by Margaret A. Hogan, C. James Taylor, Jesse May Rodroque, Hobson Woodward, Greg L. Lint, Mary T. Claffey, pp. 247, 251. Cambridge, Mass.: The Belknap Press of Harvard University Press, Copyright 2007 by the Massachusetts Historical Society.

Picture Credits

About the Author

Kem Knapp Sawyer is the author of *Anne Frank* and *Eleanor Roosevelt*, both in the DK Biography series. Her other books for children include *Freedom Calls: Journey of a Slave Girl*. She lives with her husband in Washington, D.C. They have three daughters. Learn more about the author and her work at www.kemsawyer.com.

Other DK Biographies you'll enjoy:

Marie Curie
Vicki Cobb
ISBN 978-0-7566-3831-3 paperback
ISBN 978-0-7566-3832-0 hardcover

Charles Darwin
David C. King
ISBN 978-0-7566-2554-2 paperback
ISBN 978-0-7566-2555-9 hardcover

Princess Diana
Joanne Mattern
ISBN 978-0-7566-1614-4 paperback
ISBN 978-0-7566-1613-7 hardcover

Amelia Earhart
Tanya Lee Stone
ISBN 978-0-7566-2552-8 paperback
ISBN 978-0-7566-2553-5 hardcover

Thomas Edison
Jan Adkins
978-0-7566-5207-4 paperback
978-0-7566-5206-7 hardcover

Albert Einstein
Frieda Wishinsky
ISBN 978-0-7566-1247-4 paperback
ISBN 978-0-7566-1248-1 hardcover

Benjamin Franklin
Stephen Krensky
ISBN 978-0-7566-3528-2 paperback
ISBN 978-0-7566-3529-9 hardcover

Gandhi
Amy Pastan
ISBN 978-0-7566-2111-7 paperback
ISBN 978-0-7566-2112-4 hardcover

Harry Houdini
Vicki Cobb
ISBN 978-0-7566-1245-0 paperback
ISBN 978-0-7566-1246-7 hardcover

Helen Keller
Leslie Garrett
ISBN 978-0-7566-0339-7 paperback
ISBN 978-0-7566-0488-2 hardcover

Thomas Jefferson
Jacqueline Ching
ISBN 978-0-7566-4506-9 paperback
ISBN 978-0-7566-4505-2 hardcover

Joan of Arc
Kathleen Kudlinksi
ISBN 978-0-7566-3526-8 paperback
ISBN 978-0-7566-3527-5 hardcover

John F. Kennedy
Howard S. Kaplan
ISBN 978-0-7566-0340-3 paperback
ISBN 978-0-7566-0489-9 hardcover

Martin Luther King, Jr.
Amy Pastan
ISBN 978-0-7566-0342-7 paperback
ISBN 978-0-7566-0491-2 hardcover

Abraham Lincoln
Tanya Lee Stone
ISBN 978-0-7566-0834-7 paperback
ISBN 978-0-7566-0833-0 hardcover

Nelson Mandela
Lenny Hort & Laaren Brown
ISBN 978-0-7566-2109-4 paperback
ISBN 978-0-7566-2110-0 hardcover

Mother Teresa
Maya Gold
ISBN 978-0-7566-3880-1 paperback
ISBN 978-0-7566-3881-8 hardcover

Annie Oakley
Chuck Wills
ISBN 978-0-7566-2997-7 paperback
ISBN 978-0-7566-2986-1 hardcover

Pelé
Jim Buckley
ISBN 978-0-7566-2987-8 paperback
ISBN 978-0-7566-2996-0 hardcover

Eleanor Roosevelt
Kem Knapp Sawyer
ISBN 978-0-7566-1496-6 paperback
ISBN 978-0-7566-1495-9 hardcover

George Washington
Lenny Hort
ISBN 978-0-7566-0835-4 paperback
ISBN 978-0-7566-0832-3 hardcover

Laura Ingalls Wilder
Tanya Lee Stone
ISBN 978-0-7566-4508-3 paperback
ISBN 978-0-7566-4507-6 hardcover

Look what the critics are saying about DK Biography!

"…highly readable, worthwhile overviews for young people…" —*Booklist*

"This new series from the inimitable DK Publishing brings together the usual brilliant photography with a historian's approach to biography subjects." —*Ingram Library Services*